Mad Guns Tili Romance

Mad Guns Till Romance

LeRoy Hewitt, Jr

iUniverse, Inc.
New York   Bloomington

Mad Guns Till Romance

iUniverse books may be ordered through booksellers or by contacting:

iUniverse
1663 Liberty Drive
Bloomington, IN 47403
www.iuniverse.com
1-800-Authors (1-800-288-4677)

ISBN: 978-1-4401-5607-6 (pbk)
ISBN: 978-1-4401-5608-3 (ebk)

Printed in the United States of America

iUniverse rev. date: 7/16/2009

TABLE OF CONTENTS

INTRODUCTION

"Mad Guns Till Romance," is the second book written by the author. His first book is entitled: "Crime Love & Black Pearls."

This book, " Mad Guns Till Romance," is just as exciting, if not more. Entailing rhythm, and poetic qualities.

Never before has any book revealed such knowledge of true life experiences, in part based upon fact, and fiction. Embodied with beauty, and drama. Dramatized through the heart of poetry.

The contents of this wonderful book, speaks the language of true feelings. It can stimulate the reader's heart, soul, and mind.

Bring a sense of enlightenment. Capture the imagination, through the passages of written expressions. You can enjoy, and appreciate this magnificent work, for years to come.

It gives you a look into the window of modern day poetry; a treasury of poem, and short poetic novels. Displaying the beauty of thought, and imaginative power.

There, has never been any book containing such wonderful, and exciting, short poetic novels, and poems, based upon true observations of life experiences, with a touch of fact, and fiction. Once you have read this magnificent book. It is my belief that you will agree.

ACKNOWLEDGEMENT

Giving thanks to the Lord, in heaven above, for all the wonderful blessings, and for making all things possible.

Thanks to the publisher of this wonderful book, and all the staff members, for their kindness, and assistance.

Thanks to my entire, wonderful family, for their inspiration, love, and support.

A very gracious thanks to those of you, who take the time to read this book, or any part of it. May you spread love across the would.

Across the mighty mountains,
to the wells of
the life giving
fountains.

Into a rich lovely spring,
where the humming
birds sang.

Through the darkness of night,
to the glow of
daylight.

Into the winds, at springtime
ends, where summer
begins.

It leads me through the
path of a milky way,
near the rise
of a sunny
day.

Into a world filled with
incomparable
wonders.

There behind, across the tall
snowy mountains,
yonder.

Your eyes can capture the starling

beauty, and the drama of
the sunrise. As you
whisper by.

A dazzling display, reflecting
colorful starlight
rays, along
the way.

Flickering across the sky,
a beauty to
your eyes.

The brightest star comes
clearly in
view.

As though it has eyes,
to see
you.

WILD FLOWERS
OF ARRAY

Wild flowers of array.
　　　Brings robust beauty
　　　　　To a lovely day.

Beauty to behold. The
　　　colors of the world shows,
　　　　　Flourishing across the meadows.

Spreading throughout the open
　　　Fields. Spanning atop the green
　　　　　Hills. Living beneath the sun glare,
　　　　　　　Giving fragrance to the fresh air

Wild flowers of array, their
　　　Loveliness is on display.
　　　　　Parading in harmony, as
　　　　　　　Far as the eyes can see.

Buds floating in the wind,
　　　Following springs end. To
　　　　　bring summer back again.

Across the wide open plains,
　　　The wild flowers unfolds.
　　　　　Fluttering untamed, when
　　　　　　　Ever the wind blows.

Brilliant mixture of colors, harmonize
　　　　With spring. Creating a picture of
　　　　　　Music, when the humming birds sing.

Lovely wild flowers, developed
　　　　By robust powers. Sprinkled
　　　　　　By the gentle rain shower

Staring at the moon, awaiting
　　　　Morning to come soon. To lend
　　　　　　A radiant glow, to the valleys below.

A glimpse at nature's idea,
　　　　To beautify the green fields.
　　　　　　A gentle plan, that brings
　　　　　　　　Bright colors to the land.

Adorning the hilltops, washed
　　　　By the rain drops. Skillfully
　　　　　　Inlaid, caressed by the sun rays.

As colorful birds fly. Wild
　　　　Flowers of array, take wings of
　　　　　　Beauty, before our eyes. Glowing
　　　　　　　　Beneath the radiant sky.

Blending fragrance in the
　　　　Winds, flaring along the way.
　　　　　　Wild flowers of array, stringing
　　　　　　　　Blossoms across the day.

Wild Flowers Of Array

SNAKE EYES

Snake eyes. a toss of dice.
A slight of hand.
who will lose
their life?

Lady luck, a deal is struck.
You become her
prize. A kiss of
death. Soon
you may
die.

A game of chance. A pair of
rolling bones. When
It's all over,
whom will
your soul
Belong?

Beware of queen cobra. She will
lure you into false
hope, with rising
smoke. Emanating
from burning
dope.

With a wink of her eye.
you could be living,
a poisonous
high.

A drumbeat. Beneath a black
light. Absent of
sight. The queen
cobra rises
from the
night.

Snake eyes. Appealing to the
spirits. Rendering
the flesh
weary.

Hard seats, a concrete bed.
soon your soul,
may by sleeping
with the
dead.

Backroom deals. Popping pills.
using snake eyes
to kill. Sending
forth bad luck
years.

Seemingly peaceful, into the
stare of snake
eyes. A look
can be
deceitful.

Snake eyes, blackjack, illegal
contact. All have their
impact. Who can
survive the
Stare of the
Snake
Eyes?

Lured into a trap. Soft words
over cold lips.
Lady luck
will give
you the
slip.

Snake eyes, no way to apologize.
A crawl before you
die. An empty
wish, covered
in disguise.

Snake eyes, Looking for a high.
Leaving you with
a farewell, and
a good-bye.

LOVE IS IN
THE AIR

Love is in the air,
for two, to
share.

> Whether man and
> woman, or pink
> swans in
> pairs.

It blows upon lovers,
strolling through
the summer
breeze.

> On the humming
> birds, that sang
> among the
> autumn
> leaves.

Love is in the air,
across the
rivers and
streams.

Creating sweet
memories. giving
colors, to the
midnight
dreams.

It blows in the
winter winds,
that nature
sends.

In the cool green
valleys, where
spring has
been.

It melts in the
tender hearts,
on a sunny
day.

Takes all your cares,
and troubles,
then cast
them
away.

Love is in the air,
each moment
we share.

A walk in the
park, a kiss
after
dark.

Sweeping across
the ocean,
in plain
view.

Blowing upon
stolen wishes, where
love is made
anew.   Love Is In The Air

ACROSS THE WINDS

On the wings of an Eagle, in perfect flight. Sailing across
the winds, in purple light. With wings of fire,
lighting up the night.

Into a journey that has no end, flying in a trend,
where men, nor beast. Has
ever been.

Floating on air, gliding across the sky. Purple
star light, flash before
my eyes.

Trailing behind the sunrise, on the shadow of dawn.
flying pass a milky way. To the grand
break of day.

On the wings of an Eagle, sailing across the winds.
Through a passage, that can never be
traveled again.

Reaching toward the heavens above,
to an Angel with wings
of love.

Graceful as a Gazelle, leaping through the air.
Carrying good wishes, that only a brave
Heart can bear.

Into the door of time, with love on my mind. Sailing
above the summer showers, across the
Rainbow flowers.

My heart bursting with cheer, deep into the atmosphere.
Gleaming purple light, flickering
through the night.

Feeling free, sweeping across the sea. A dazzling
sunburst, sent an exciting rush. In a day
of fun, shield by the sun.

I could feel the sunshine, see the blue sky smile.
The night stars came near, to give
the purple light,
to my eye.

Across the Winds.
Embracing
the night,
In purple light.

SUMMER KISSES

Summer kisses,
is what my
heart misses.

In the winter
cold, before
the spring
unfolds.

Your soft embrace,
and the smile
upon your
face.

The gentle touch
of your lips.
The tenderness
of your fingertips.

A love in kind,
is what we
find.

Summer kisses,
beneath the
night skies.

With the love
that sparkles
in your
eyes.

With each season,
blooms a new
reason.
For summer kisses
to warm our hearts,
before the cold
season
starts.

With the romance
of spring, sweet
summer kisses,
will make
our hearts
sing.

Rich summer kisses.
after the spring
is done.

Bring warmth to
our hearts,
beneath the
winter
sun.

Summer kisses, before
the fall of autumn.
Goes a long ways,
to warm the
coldest
winter
days.

GENTLE RAIN

Softly comes the
gentle rain.
Touching upon
my windowpane.

With its pita pat
sound alight.
Bringing closure
to my sleepless
night.

Refreshing the
moonless night.
Beneath the star
faded light.

Gentle rain
showers, that
falls for hours.
So it remains.

Creeping quietly
into the day. So
came the gentle
rain.

That washed
my blues
away.

Sweet sounds
of gentle rain
drops.

That trickle upon
my dwelling
top.

A comforting
sound. Softly,
the rain came
down.

My dreams
were entertained,
when the gentle
rain came.

My head lay
upon my pillow.
My ears listen
to the musical
drizzle,

When the gentle
rain came.
So clean and
plain.

Gentle rain
of delight.
Falling upon
my sleepless
night.

CATCH ME IF YOU CAN

Fast on my feet. For
   the gold I compete.
   I won't stop running
        until the day is complete.
        Catch
           Me
              If
            You can.

A run of a lifetime.
   a race that I must finish.
   My body is fit, ready as any.

Running through the heart
   of time. I won't stop short
   of the finish line. For this
      race I strive to win.
      Catch
        Me
           If
             You can.

Speed is given to the elite,
fleet of feet. Swift as the
   wind. Hard, will I compete.

For the golden
trophy, that
await at the end.
Catch

Me

If
You can.

Reaching for the stars.
Aiming for the sky. My heart
is bursting with pride. Who can
pass me by? Going for the win.
Catch

Me

If
You can.

I will hurdle over troubles. Burst
through walls of resentment. Yet,
I will press on for the prize, that
captured my eye. Nothing
can get under my skin.
Catch

Me

If
You can.

Running at high speed,
flashing through the blowing
        winds. Who can intercede? Running
            with the elite. Refusing to retreat.
                Catch
                        Me
                                If
                        You can.

Like a lightning strike. That
touches down beneath The
        sky. With fiery wings that fly.
        A wild ride to the journey's end.
                Catch
                        Me
                                If
                        You can.

At the end of the day. When
the twilight is falling, and the
        nightingales are calling.

Running in the wind, that
    a day bring. Sailing through
            the air, if you dare. To the end of spring.
                Catch
                        Me
                                If
                        You can.

The days are long.
Nevertheless I press on.
Racing with the winds.
Catch
Me
If
You can.

LOVE EMBRACE

Love embrace, a
beautiful face.
Kisses and
hugs, sustain
true love.

Sunny skies, love is
in your eyes.
A kind word;
never a
good-bye.

Sleepless nights;
romantic moon
light. Living
dreams; a lady
in white.

Love embrace, true
love stays.
A heart of
Gold; sunny
days.

Into the night,
love glows bright.
True romance, a
heart will
advance.

Spring is in the
air, flowers
everywhere.

Dazzled by the
rain showers,
that brings
loving powers.

Love embrace,
a kind heart
gets paid.
Golden rewards,
as ocean waves.

Love Embrace

SMOKING GUN

A shot rang out. He who cling to his possession, will surely be without. A man stands along. The pull of a trigger, then a life is gone.

A Smoking Gun, man on the run. Robbing and killing, in a quest for fun. Given nothing to learn. Who is the guilty one?

A flash in the night; a spark of light. A holdup, to fill his cup, with money, for the love of his honey. A modern day crime, seeking to avoid prison time.

A Smoking Gun. A gift of flowers, for the control of powers. Using a gun in the midnight hours. To get ahead, no matter who lay dead.

Smoking Gun, man on the run. Killing to get a chance, for the thrill of romance.

A standoff; no time to pause. A life will be lost. He who holds the Smoking Gun, will possess it all. Until he falls

Taking aim; blasting rounds, someone will surely go down. Smoke rises high, blinding his eyes. Who will be the one to die?

Led astray; trying to get away; someone will have to pay. Commit a crime, do the hard time.

A Smoking Gun, man on the run. A life cut short, with

a gun he bought. His life is a waste, living just a few days. In a quest for fun, beneath the eyes of the sun.

The glow of sunset, melts into the twilight. A fight, a hail of gunfire blazing in the night. He who stands behind the Smoking Gun, disappears from sight.

No time to relax, got to watch his back. Man on the run, a hard lesson he must learn.

Packing heat; robbing at will; just to get food to eat. Shoot to kill, was part of the deal. Learned in a street life drill.

No time to play, or listen to what the wise men say. Programmed to blast anyone, who gets in his way.

Smoking Gun, man on the run. Quick to rob, jacking cars. Soon he will be living behind prison bars.

Living in the fast lane, with gun in hand, looking for lost romance.

Racing in the night; searching for the daylight. Hiding beneath the telling sky, with tears in his eyes.

Jail time, not far behind. A prison cell, his life will be compelled.

Going down to hell, for the men, whom he fell. The truth they will tell.

The Devil is waiting at the gate, to show him the way, and the price he must pay.

Smoking Gun, man on the run. His life comes to an end. Nothing to spend, but to pay for his sins. Nothing is left, but to die a quick death.

Smoking Gun,
man on the run.

ANGELS OF SONG

Hear the Angels sang, in the voice of spring,
that only Angels can bring. The kind
of music that we all love,
that flows from the
Heavens above.

It echo upon the winds. Sending
music across the sea, in
a springtime melody.

It comes alive on a beautiful spring day.
as wings of the Angels flutter
above and below,
when the fine
winds blow.

Songs with lyrics, that only the eyes of the
heart can see. Blending the sweet
sound of music, that will last
an eternity.

A perfect blend, with lights of purple colors,
rising in the winds. Songs of good
wishes, reflecting their spirits,
uplifting the weary.

Like diamonds in the sky, the Angels
of song take wings and fly. With
a tender melody, blending
with soft harmony.

Hear the gentle lullaby, floating on air.
When the Angels of song takes to
the sky. Embracing the stars
with an Angel's smile.

Sweet songs of loveliness, so clear and pure.
Angels of song, singing sweet music,
for our ears to hear. Piercing
the heart with a Heavenly
cheer.

CRYING EYES

The tears in your
eyes. Show the
pain that burns
in your
heart.

Since the love
you shared has
been broken
apart.

A sobering cry.
After the last
good-bye.

A tear drop,
awaiting the
falling rain
to stop.

Crying eyes,
true love has
passed you
by.

Eyes made sad,
by the love
you once
had.

Your sunshine has
disappeared.

Only faded love,
is left for your
heart to
feel.

Dark clouds,
have set in
for a rainy
day.

Your crying eyes,
trying to wash
the pain
away.

A wishing well,
filled with dreams.
where lovers
come to
play.

Your heart can
wish upon a
star, to bring
back a lovely
day.

Blue skies, comes
alive. To bring sparkle
to your
crying
eyes.

Tears drops, will
subside. When
your crying eyes,
began to
smile.

                    Your Crying Eyes

BREAKOUT

Behind faded prison walls, is where I was sent. To do hard time, for a crime I didn't commit.

For years! I have been living in the darkness of hell. Slowly dying in a cold prison cell.

It is raw, and hardcore here. Whether in solitary confinement, or walking the yard. At any moment, you can be killed, by a makeshift weapon, such as a sharp piece of steel.

Cons that are lucky enough, to get out of here, by filing successful appeals, are smart enough, not to come back again. Aware of how hard it had been.

My mind continue to fad. I have to struggle harder than ever, to get through the long rugged days. I have filed endless appeals, but the judge has failed to adhere.

For years! I have been living behind the cold stone walls. Now, with all my might, soon after midnight, or there about. I will rise up, and breakout! Along with my cellmate, before the next daybreak.

Busting out of a place, where grow men weep. where you may die in your sleep.

Where a pack of cigarettes is pay, for a hole, to be put in your head, while you lay in bed.

Busting out of a place, where hate and crime is real. Where at any moment, you stand a chance of being drilled. Chinked with a carved out knife, or a cold piece of steel.

The sky is mad tonight. The thunder is growling aloud. I have giving money to guards to burn my prison file.

The lightning is making fierce strikes all around, across the prison grounds. As if it is reaching for someone to cut down.

The hard rain, is pouring water everywhere. As though it is trying to wash away the blood stains, that align the prison yard. where many men souls, have been ripped apart.

The armed guards were pacing, back and forth near the cellblock. It was eleven o'clock. Tonight! Was the night. Whether I live or die. It was time to breakout. Tonight! One way or another, I will say my last good-bye. My stay here, will be just pie in the sky.

"Lights out prison boys. Shake your bodies, and put them into your hard prison beds." Is what the guard said.

We quietly removed the picture, from the mouth of the tunnel, that we had made in the prison wall. The cement around the edge of the narrow escape hole, started to fall. We pause for awhile, with knives by our side, but no one came by.

Quickly! We hit the tunnel, crawling on our bellies like reptiles; or snakes, coming from the lake. We moved swiftly, trying to make it outside the prison walls before daybreak.

We could hear the roaring thunder bellowing in the night. Clashing aloud, hovering over the prison site. We escaped through the tunnel, and came out near the gun tower, under heavy rain showers.

Mad rain continued to beat upon the prison grounds, but it didn't slow us down, as the spotlights scanned the prison all around.

With a makeshift knife, my cellmate chinked
the guard, that patrolled the bottom of the gun tower.
Attacking hard.

His body went limp, and dropped down, stretched across the wet prison ground, beneath the hard pouring rain. There, his body could be found. Drenched in blood stains. Wet from the falling rain.

We had to stop him from making phone calls, or our effort would be lost. As we scaled the high prison wall. We dropped to the other side. Eluding the other guards eyes. We were ready to make our getaway, beneath the cloudy skies.

It was well past midnight; the dark moon withheld its light. Then, suddenly! The two armed guards standing atop the gun tower made us. There! They started fussing and cursing.

"Stop right there, and don't move your feet, or you both will be dead meat." We ran for cover behind the prison walls. We knew whatever they had to do, they would bring it all.

We headed toward the near by woods. The guns from the tower were pumping. We could hear lead falling near our feet, but we kept on thumping.

We stormed into the dark woods. Men with rifles, shotguns, and blood thirsty dogs, came after us. Making lot of fuss, fast as they could, we knew they would.

They came out of the night. Running with guns, dogs, and flashlights. If they had caught up with us, the powerful jaws of the blood thirsty dogs, would have ripped us apart, running after dark. Cut us into piece with a vicious dog bite, running in the night.

They were having a difficult time, locating our where about. The rain covered our tracks; we doubled back.

We headed for the bus that was parked outside the prison site. The driver had mounted a special compartment beneath the bus. He had extorted money from the both of us. We raced through the night, taking flight.

We crawled under the bus, before the chain gang were brought out. It was a tight squeeze, but we moved about, fitted our bodies in, coming out of the freezing winds.

We would have to hold on tightly, for dear life, with all our might. When the prison bus whisk down the freeway, in the early break of day.

Looking from beneath the bus. I could see the feet of the chain gang, as they came. Men in a loop, wearing black work boots. They were all shackled and chained, linked together, moving in a single file, through the stormy weather.

"Everybody on the bus. No talking ,or you will be walking. I don't want to hear nothing. Do you hear what I say? Let's get on the way." Proclaimed the armed guard.

The engine started. Soon we would be departing. Smoke, and gas fumes filled the small compartment beneath the bus. I thought that the fumes would consume the both of us.

I could barely breathe. Then, when the bus began to leave, along came a breeze. The smoke dissipated. We held on tightly, to the heated iron rails, as the bus rolled along the prison trail.

Our hands grew exceedingly tired, but we could not let go, or we would fall, and surely die. We had to withstand the wind, rain, and dust. If we lost control, the big wheels would run over us.

We arrived at a work site for the chain gang. The early morning was pouring rain. Hard calluses had grown inside our hands.

"Okay boys, let's get off the bus, and move some logs, like you did yesterday in the heavy fog." Is what the guard said, as the chain gang was led.

We slowly removed ourselves from beneath the bus. The chain gang was gone. It were just the two of us. As I raised my eyes. I could see the chain gang, running away in the rain. Some had freed themselves with guns in hand.

Shots were fired; deadly fights broke out. Stone cold prisoners were running about. Men laid dead beneath the pouring rain. Others were running across the plain, as if they were insane.

The prison guards were stretched across the wet ground. They had been gunned down, by men of the chain gang. To many men had been killed. I stopped to say a prayer. Their bodies laid still.

We headed out across the open field. From the time of our breakout, before now, only one man had been killed. By our hands. Only one man had to died. It was the gun toting guard that was chinked in the side, back at the prison site. No one was meant to die. May his family say, their last good bye.

The day had faded. We had completed the plans of the breakout. Running in the heart of darkness, into the black night. The sun had sunk. As we slogged through the brutal swamp.

We paused awhile, to eat pieces of bitter plants to stay alive.
We took flight, through the darkest winter nights.

Life in the wilderness had been cruel. We scarcely made it
through. Our bodies were freezing cold. We lit a fire that
burned high. Than, the rain came, and the fire died.

The flames disappeared into the wet winds. Then, came the
cold air, creeping in.

We could hear the sound of howling coyotes, echo through
the dark woods. We struggled to get a little shuteye, when
ever we could.

Across the grassy swamp, the fierce wind was racing. We
pressed on, no time were we wasting.

As time went by. My cellmate caught a fatal illness, and
died. For him, I couldn't hold back the tears from my eyes,
before we said our final good bye.

My life has been overwhelmed by terror and grief. Since our
breakout, I do feel a scene of relief.

My mind has been scarred, and the wounds can't be healed.
As I traveled toward the city, through a tall grassy field.

I now live my life as a vagabond. A fugitive on the run.
I live in the back woods, under bridges, and freeways for
days. I roam the slums, and trust no one.

At times I go without food for days. I let my beard grow long, to hide my face. I drank black water, and eat from garbage cans. Living a life as a runagate man.

At any time you may see me, when you go out to empty the trash. I may be wearing a long beard, with a sack on my back. Wearing dirty clothes, sometimes my shoes may have holes.

I have been without a woman for a longtime. I'm willing to steal, for romance, for just one moment of a thrill. It's a lonely life, but for this type of freedom, I must pay the price.

I must be moving on. My eyes can now see the sun that shines bright. The moon, and the stars that decorate the night.

A farewell! I am free from the prison cell, but my life, is still a living hell.

PLAYING THE
GAME OF LOVE

Playing the game
of love. When the
stars came, with
The summer rain.

Running in the night,
looking for the light.
shooting stars above,
falling in love.

Waiting for the warm
sun, and the wings
of light to come,
from the flame
of dawn.

Playing by the rules,
true love will never
lose. Destine to win
your love, by the
brightest stars
above.

Playing the game
of love. Running
through to rain.
my eyes for you,
will never change.

Walking in the park,
playing after dark.
Eyes of night,
driven by the
moonlight.

The nights are cool.
Playing the love
game is what
we chose.

If I lose your love,
It will be as
Living, with a
heart of
fools.

Laughter in the
sunshine, eyes
are never
crying.

A stroll in the night,
arms holding you
tight. Bringing
sparks of romance,
before the
morning light.

In the game of love,
flows magic
kisses, and
mystic
hugs.

Infatuation, games
of sensation.
Running with
the wind, love
has no
end.

Singing a melody,
over coming
jealousy.

Dancing to a dreamy
tune, waiting
for love to
bloom.

Glowing eyes, flying
high. In stormy
weather, on wings
of a feather.
Love will
get you
by.

Playing the love
game, romantic
nights still
remains.

Counting the stars
above, soon our
hearts will be
falling in
love.

Whispering for a
kiss, true love
won't be
missed.

My love for
you, grows
in plain
view.

Starry eyes, a gentle
smile. A kiss in the
night, two hearts
beats with delight.

Timeout, your love
I can't be without,
if ever in
doubt.

A cry for a smile,
raindrops for
blue skies.

Ask why, someone
lips be telling
lies.

Colors from the rainbow,
coming to you, bearing
love that's true. It
takes two. As
sure as the
morning
dew.

I made a play, for you
to stay. You came
with a flair, with
wings of a love
affair.

A soft love song, can
bring gentle rain.
Ease a heart of
pain, ignite
love flames.

Playing to win your
dreams, beneath
the stars above,
all in the
name of
love.

In the quietness of
night, beneath
the starry
light.

With the moon glowing
high above. We
play the game
of love.

Truth or dare,
love is in
the air.

Hands on the wishing
well, playing the
game of kiss
and tell.

Hide and go seek.
Counting down
before the eyes
begin to
peep.

Searching to find,
that love of mine.
Trying not to
miss, holding
out for a
kiss.

Beneath the sky
above. Playing
the game
of love.

THE MOVIE QUEEN

Hail to the Movie Queen. She spent
her time on the silver screen.
Came to life in a
romantic love
scene.

She articulated her script.
Leading men loved
to kiss her
lips.

She perfected her lines. Delivered
them precisely when
it was time.

Her appearance was always in demand.
It is easy to understand. She was
the leading lady. Whom
always got the
leading man.

She sang like a nightingale. In a scene
across the western trail, many
movie tickets would sell.
She played her
part well.

In stylish wardrobe, for pictures she
posed. When ever she presented
herself in person, her fans
would greet her
in droves.

She was truly admired by gals
and guys. Who gazed
upon her beauty
with pride.

Many men ask to marry
her. She was never
out of character.

A sleek look, she read
romantic books.

Eloquently, she gave a performance
in a love scene, that earned her
the title, as the
Movie Queen.

PIRATES OF THE SEA SKINNER

The days were long; the nights were bloody. We were the pirates that sailed the high sea aboard the ship called the "Sea Skinner." We would aim, shoot and kill, with skill. When our hands were steady.

We were the most fearsome and treacherous pirates that ever sailed the South Pacific. We sailed the African Coast, to the Indian Ocean. If any fighting was to be done, we would set it in motion.

If you got in our way, we would cut your face, signifying that you were living in your last days.

The Sea Skinner was managed by Captain Blake.
A rugged man, who seemed to always have a violent plan. He killed for thrills. Poured whiskey and wine down his throat; overflowing onto his beard. We took treasures of diamonds and pearls, silver and gold from around the world.

We sailed the Caribbean Sea. During that time it was called the sea of gold. Because of the large amount of gold that passed through it. This is what we were told.

 Our flag was bones in red. Men who set eyes on it have bled, many lay dead.

We owned the reputation as the blood thirsty killing machine. We lived aboard the sea Skinner. The roughest and toughest pirates that any one had ever seen, and said to be just as mean.

We were said to be murderous, and cutthroats, who roamed the sea from coast to coast. Killing, robbing ships, and burning boats.

We ripped men with the sword as they felled, and staggered. Slashed, and cut by the blade of daggers.

Blasting enemy ships with hot firepower, in the hard fought standoff hours. Unleashing bloody attacks, and initiating rugged fights, far into the black night. Raiding, and taking everything that were in sight.

Many men died, some tried to run and hide. You could hear the thundering battle echo throughout the high sea. As we upheld the pirate's creed. Fire and smoke filled the air. No man life, would we spare. We took the richest treasures, refusing to share.

We were men who robbed, stole and killed. Possessing speed and skill. Thieves who gave other pirates a reason to flee, across the hostile sea.

The day had shut it's gates to the evening sun. we were geared up to take a run. The black night had spread across the deep waters. It was time to board the Sea Skinner, and shove off. Tonight, someone path to glory, would soon be clogged.

We were preparing to ease out to sea, in the quietness of night. In search of other ships to rob, and men to kill. Like the wild beasts that roam the dark jungle, and the grassy fields. In search of prey, on a hot summer day.

Suddenly! My eyes spotted Captain Blake, coming toward the Sea Skinner, with a dozen men. They staggered drunkenly, barely able to stand on their feet, headed for the fleet.

They carried barrel of whiskey and wine. It was nearing the set sail time. Peasants were shanghaied when intoxicated, and dragged aboard the ship for cheap labor, in which they participated.

"Get up there you slobs. It is time to hit the high sea. My belly thirst for blood, and the night is young and free," the Captain said, as the drunken men were led.

Violent weather hung heavily over the sea. The night sky was not smiling, a bad moon was rising.

I was a young man, who went by the name of "Troy." The way of life I failed to understand. I was influenced by older men, who told wild tails of good times, sailing the high sea. As time went by, I thought one of those hard nose men, was how I wanted my life to be, sailing the deep blue waters, on the sea.

Captain Blake, once told me. 'the reason he named the ship, the Sea Skinner, is because we live a life at sea. Similar to hunters that go out, and kill wild animals. Skin them, and hang the carcasses out to dry, or to die.'

He went on to say, 'the crew aboard the Sea Skinner, do the same. By robbing, and stealing from the enemy, and hang their souls out to dry, until they die.'

We boarded the Sea Skinner, headed out to sea. Plowing through the black waters in the darkness of night, as the moon give us light.

Tonight we will be matching wits with a ship called the "Dragon." The crew had stole more silver and gold, than any pirates roaming the sea. This we had been told.

With fiery spirit, the flames of determination, and desire had been lit. We would locate the Dragon that possessed the treasure, then we would take it.

Somehow, we had eluded any bounty that could have been placed on our heads. A huge bounty had been placed on the crew of the Dragon instead. Huge bets, we were about to collect.

"Listen up!" The Captain said. "My name is not black beard, and many men have I killed. I eat raw fish, and swallow the bones. If you get in my way, I will put a sword to your neck, and from your shoulders, your head, will soon be gone."

"We are after the ship called the "Dragon." My hate for that crew is deep to the bone. They snatched a treasure right out of my hand. Whatever they are carrying now. To me, it belong."

"I'm mad! Tonight we will defect them, and send the Dragon to the bottom of hell, for an eternity. There, it will dwell. We will take a fierce stand, their fate, we hold in the palms of our hand."

We sailed the deep blue sea through the eternal darkness of night. We sailed beneath a dazzling sunburst, and at the roaring sea we curst. We sailed the high sea for days. Searching for the pirates aboard the Dragon, with blood on our face.

Suddenly! We spotted the Dragon plowing through the hostile waters up ahead. They spotted our bones in red flag, then quietly they fled.
The fog had just started to roll in. We could barely see the sales blowing in the wind. We swiftly moved in close. Preparing for the battle that was about to unfold.

Tonight, We would mount a fierce fight. It was as if, we could hear the sea cry, for the men who would die. Dark clouds, covered the eyes of the sky.

If we could setup an ambush, we would get our wish. We knew this chance would not last.
We tried to sink the Dragon before the night pass.

Our faces had been scorched by the burning sun. We geared up for a fierce fight, when the Dragon began to run, then out came the fire and the big guns.

By their surprise we unleashed a cannon ball strike, the wind was at our back. Huge flames ignited aboard the vessel. The Dragon was crippled, as the ship plowed through hostile waters.

Black smoke from the Dragon billowed high, toward
the night sky. We vigorously pursued, as the Dragon was
looking for a place to hide.

From the bowels of the Sea Skinner, we once again
unleashed heavy loads of firepower, upon the notorious
Dragon. In a quest to sink her, to the bottom of the sea.
Hot on her trail, so were we.

We got off round after rounds, of flying artillery. The ship
refused to go down. We gave it our all, the crew aboard
the Dragon lost us in the fog. It sailed crippled toward the
lighthouse tower, then came the rain showers.

Massive ocean waves, slowed the speed of our ship. For this
reason the Dragon might have been saved. The night calmed
the high sea. we turned to sail away, into another day.

We landed on an undisturbed Island, inhabited by wild beasts.
We could hear their roar as we reached the sea shore beach.

We spent time resting. Setting around campfires telling tails
of old pirates stories, of the days of glory. Getting intoxicated
on whiskey and wine. Gambling and dancing, as we passed
the time.

We got restless, time was moving fast. The golden daggers
of sunrays cut through the dark sky. Cold rain hovered
nearby, awaiting to fall upon the ship, in a grueling day at
sea. Beneath the eyes in the sky.

We have left many souls buried at sea. It wasn't nothing personal, that's just the way life turned out to be. The sea yielded richest that were up for grab, and every pirate would try to harvest the huge treasures, that were unmeasured.

As time went by, once again we took to the sea. We sailed swiftly, plowing into the winds at high speed. In search of the ship with the biggest treasure, as we would proceed. In an instant, we seemed to be lost, entrance in diamonds, and golden light, amid a stretch of the South Pacific in the dead of night.

We traveled through the hostile sea, that had swallowed thieves, and stolen ships, as we poured whiskey passed our lips.

Sailing the Sea Skinner to an Island, where no human eyes, ever wanted to see, is the way it appeared to be. The night was falling, as the beasts were calling, and along were we.

Tired and exhausted, we would choose to sleep, rather then eat. We broke out bottles of rum. The men moved in haste, just to get a taste.

We were drunken with women and wine. Our energy was high. We spotted a pirate ship sailing by, with flashing lights that lit up the sky.

It was the Royal Palace. A ship owned by King Deleon. It carried the richest treasures, unmeasured. It also, possessed the biggest guns, that had sunk many ships, and sent others on the run.

We would desperately try, to take them out before daybreak. From the claws of the Sea Skinner, only a few ships had escaped.

We were prepared to unleash a fierce battle, to bring the treasure before our eyes. A huge cargo of diamond, pearls, silver and gold, we would divide. Take no blind chance; grab women for a time of romance.

Dark clouds rested on the distant waters, as if awaiting our arrival. Holding our fate of death, or survival.

We raised our bones in red flag. We were men at sea, who seemed to have gone mad. We launched a fierce attack, but the Royal Palace fought back.

We unleashed stones of fire, mounting a hard fight. We blasted them with loads of firepower, attacking in the midnight hour.

The enemy fired back, with a heavy attack. Our vessel burst into flames. Out of nowhere, The cannon ball came.

The Sea Skinner was burning fast, we had met our match at last. Our ship was shattered, we were now fighting to survive. Our fleet plowed through the high tides, as we struggled to stay alive.

Violence filled the air. We were in despair. Men were blasted over the ship's sides, plunging into the sea. There, many men died.

The Sea Skinner was sinking fast, as we tried to sail away, into another day. The Royal Palace moved ahead. Our crew members laid dead. Buried at the bottom of the deep waters. Never again would their eyes see. The remains of the mighty Sea Skinner, will always be, buried at sea.

The Royal Palace had superior firepower. The Sea Skinner failed to reach the lighthouse tower, swallowed up by the sea. I managed to escaped, and swam to the sea shore. Barely standing on my feet, I was tired and beat.

My body was torn. Horrible thoughts raced through my mind. Fire and smoke filled the day, as the sea winds carried it away.

I knew the times of the Sea Skinner, would not last. A strange voice I heard, when we drank wine mingled with enemy blood.

Death would be swift, and move in fast. Only I was left alive, when the crew of the Sea Skinner died.

So long to the crew, and the mighty Sea Skinner. Whiskey and wine, we drank for good times. So long to the sea waves, and the winds that blew upon our face. When the Sea Skinner sailed, the high sea, in her glory days.

SUMMER DREAMS

Summer dreams, of days beneath
    The green palm trees. Refreshed
        By the cool summer breeze.

Dreams of cool summer evenings.
    Where the air is delightful, and
        The calmness is pleasing.

Dreams of beautiful romance,
    Of early spring. When the birds
        Of colorful music began to sang.

Dreams of summertime fun, that
    Spout beneath the summer sun.
        Left behind by angels of wings.

With the joy that summer brings
    Summer Dreams, when the sun
        Rays of light, melts the evening
            Shade, Into the twilight.

Summer dreams, of the brightest
    Sunrise, shining pearly light
        Across the clear restless sky.

Fresh days of cool summer air,
    Left behind by the summer rain
        Showers. Extended to the
            Midnight hours.

Summer dreams, of the day
    We met. When we strolled
        Beneath the summer sunset.

Summer dreams, of springtime
    Flowers, of a colorful display.
        That comes alive on a beautiful
            Summer day.

Summer dreams, of a carefree
    Night. When we danced
        Beneath the shadow of the
            Soft moonlight.

Wishing the summer dreams
    True, for the one, and only you.

LOVE IS IN
THE NIGHT

Love is in the night.
　　　　With the sound of
　　　　　　music, piercing
　　　　　　　　romantic sites.

Love songs, floating
　　　　　　on air, when the night
　　　　　　　　is young and fair.

A touch of gentleness,
　　　　　　embracing the winds.
　　　　　　　　When lovely dreams,
　　　　　　　　　comes breezing in.

Love is in the night.
　　　　　Flying in midair,
　　　　　　when the moon
　　　　　　　is bright.

In the shooting stars, climbing
　　　　　the heights. Falling away from
　　　　　the sky, taking wing to fly. Bringing
　　　　　　　stardust to our eyes.

When we dance, on the
　　　　seashore. Bare footing
　　　　　　in the warm sand.

Love is in the night.
                    Giving colors to the
                         stars, that paints
                              the sky bright.

When the milky ways, makes
                    for charming words to say.
                         in a soft voice, before
                              the break of day.

Love is in the night.
                    When tender arms
                         are holding
                              you tight.

When the rising moon,
                    blends soon. With the
                         shinny sea that glows,
                              before the day unfolds.

Born out of the twilight.
                    When the galaxy of stars,
                         bring sparkles before our eyes.

Spread them across the
                    quiet waters, with a
                         big surprise.

Love is in the night.
                    Glowing with the moon
                         and stars. Shinning a
                              crystal bright.

The stars, lights up with a
    radiant shine. Making it
        easy for our eyes to find.

With a romantic light, and
    a galaxy of stars, that
        create such a lovely sight.

Where the stardust
    lay. Embracing
        the milky way.

Among the shooting stars, that
    flashes across the sky. Bringing
        a lovely sight to our eyes.

Love is in the night.
    Embracing our dreams, and
        the lovely sites, that our eyes have
        seen. Where the starlight beams.

Shinning bright, giving light.
    Blending with the moon, and with
        our love, that has bloomed.

CHASING THE RAINBOW

Chasing the rainbow, on a Sunday
  afternoon. Seeking to contain it,
    before the birth of the moon.

Gazing upon rings of colors, from
  my windowsill. Racing across the
    fresh green fields, through the Valleys
      I go. Following the trail left in the winds,
        by the wise old crow.

The colors are bright, sparkles in
  the light. Glowing before the
    twilight, affixed to paint the night.

Chasing the rainbow, through the
  green meadows below. Within the
    fresh water springs, is where the bright,
      colors may flow.

Born amid the rain showers, with
  magical power. It paints
    the air, a rainy day sends. Evading
      the chillness, by the cold east winds.

Over the mountains, and across the
  sea. There is a rainbow that's painted
    just for me. A thrill, cheer, coloring
      the atmosphere. A rainbow that flies,
        in the distant sky.

Suspended in air, with a colorful flare.
   Rhythm in motion, across the ocean.
         With colors that appear to be, painting
                        the deep blue sea.

When the rain came. It went passed
   my windowpane, into the open plain.
         There, it must have settled, when the
               day was mellow. Leaving a path of
                     red, blue, and a shade of yellow.

Where did the rainbow go?
         My eyes must know,
               Who can tell me so?
                     Chasing the rainbow.

MAD GUNS
FOR ROMANCE

Mad guns for romance. Hungry for love, gunning for a kiss, or just a hug.

They will do anything for love. Curse the stars above. Spill innocent blood, for just a thrill. Men they will kill.

Who can understand, the killing of a man? For the love of a woman, or just a chance, to hold her hand.

His heart is at risk, by the love he now miss. The loss of his woman, a gun he now enlist.

New love he demands, living in the sands of romance. A heart of greed, waiting to expand.

He will carryout a deadly plan,
with guns blazing in hand, just to be her only man.

Become obsessed, to accomplish her request. Rob and steal, driven by the mad love, his cold heart feel.

A kiss from her ruby red lips. Her claws digs deep, into his heart; she has a firm grip.

Guns, guts, and blood, he promised her the world. Laced with diamond and pearls.

She walks with elegance. Speaks soft words, like none he has ever heard. Keeping his mind, obsessed with crime.

By the look in her eyes, she packs a deadly surprise. Women have cried, and men have died.

With her gentle kiss, and a lovely smile. The mad guns for romance, will never say good bye.

Living on a leash, walking by her side. With a killer's life style, he is bound to die.

Living in a trance, taking a deadly chance. Who can understand? The guns in the sands of romance.

Lured into thinking that crime pays, to keep a smile on her face. Spilling innocent blood, within his mad world.

His body is strong, but his mind is weak. Lost and confused by the woman he keep.

Running in the night, wrong or right. Mad guns for romance, got you in their sight.

Like a wild beast, that stalks his prey. Prowling the night, before the break of day.

With the sight of a night owl, he's looking for someone to devour. any evil deed, his heart allows.

Wearing rhinestone, whistling a forgotten song. Living his life all wrong, killing for a happy home.

With rock hard arms, and strong broad shoulders. He holds onto a 9-milameter, and a Mac-10, tossing care to the wind.

The look in his eyes is bone chilling. With bloodstains of men, his guns have been killing.

Unleashing assaults with lightning speed, for the love of his woman, trying to meat her needs. Killing to succeed.

Let him in your home, you are living in a danger zone. Oust and dethroned

Mad guns for romance, living hard, till death do you part.

Getting intoxicated, rarely sober. Get in his way, the party is over.

His criminal mind is set in stone. Behind prison walls, is where he belong.

Standing tough, his guns makes lot of fuss. Mad guns for romance, you cannot trust.

His head is filled with violent dreams. His intentions are harsh, and mean.

Brandishing his weapons with a criminal mind. Holding onto borrowed time. Drilling bullets of lead, living on the edge.

With bloody assaults, trouble is all he brought. Sending running tears, throughout the pages of years.

Living in a nightmare, hanging on a love affair. Bearing broken dreams, without a hope, or a prayer.

He dresses his woman in the finest clothes.
A diamond ring, he has proposed.

Still! Her eyes searches for another. This! His heart will soon discover.

Sleeping with his gun readily cocked, his future awaits, inside a cellblock.

Committing crime, for a mate. Soon he will be living behind high walls, and steel gates. Doing time, for his bloody crimes.

Headed, for the death penalty, a loss of all sanity. Mad guns will die, executioner style.

Mad Guns For Romance

WHEN THE NIGHT
IS YOUNG

After the fading of the sun,
        When the twilight is done.
            I hear a quiet song.
                    When the
                    Night is young.

The evening will pass. The
        Sunset will melt away at last.
            The stars will come out first.
                    Then the moon bursts upon the
                        scene, when sprung.
                            When the
                            Night is young.

The air is fresh, and clean.
        The street lights brighten
            The scene. The bells of newly
                Born sounds, will then be rung.
                    When the
                    Night is young.

Soft music will take wings
        Upon the wind. Sending
            Lovers to delightful places,
                They have never been. Humming
                    A melody of a new found song.
                        When the
                        Night is young.

Curious eyes reveal a surprise,
When stars began to align the
Sky. Then comes a hello before a
Good-bye, where romance is strong.
When the
Night is young.

The face of the sun will look away,
At the close of the day. The night will
Be fair, with sweetness in the air. Into the
Bright street lights. Lovers will be drawn.
When the
Night is young.

The stars will decorate the night
Bring down the brightest lights.
Beneath the sky, whence they are hung.
When the
Night is young.

Lovers stroll along the cool lakes,
Before the full moon awakes. In the
Mildness of the night, they seem to belong.
When the
Night is young.

Along the seashore, resting by day,
And playing by night. Dancing the
Stars away, with wine and song.
When the
Night is young.

SNOWFLAKES

See the dancing snowflakes. That
flies from the nestling sky.
Light and fluffy, as they
Float before your
Eyes.

See the birth of the fluttering snowflakes.
That falls near the winter lake. The
Feathery snowflakes,
That thrives when
Winter awake.

Cold crystal snowflakes. Kisses the
Winds before daybreak. Falling
Freely in the afternoon,
Glittering with rays,
Of a full
Moon.

Softly, the icy snowflakes, floats on air.
Falling in single, triplet or pairs.
Trickling downward through
The twilight. Dancing
In the night.

Hold a cold snowflake gently
In hand. Feel it at finger
Tip, touch it for
Chance.

Slowly fallen snowflakes, that makes
Cold, the atmosphere.
Plays about the
Windowsills.

Creating wintertime beauty.
Melts away, then
Reappear on
A winter
Day.

See the dancing snowflakes.

THE BEGGAR

Up town, down town; people all around.
Window shopping, never stopping. Listening to the street
sounds.

Racing through traffic, barely reaching the streets; old shoes
on my feet. Begging for food to eat; looking for a place to
sleep.

Screaming sidewalks, ears are deaf to the words I speak. On
any given day, I struggle to find my way.

Faces wearing frowns. Don't want me around. Staring from a
distance, as my eyes searches for a place, to set my body down,
wasting needed pounds.

A hand extending; angels descending, zooming about the
day. Cloudy thoughts racing through my brain; I have no
place to stay.

Politician wearing the crowns, showing me the way out of
town. Having drinks inside the lounge. Tonight, I will be
making my bed, on the cold hard ground.

Whose to blame? I am not ashamed. Tomorrow my life will
still be the same.

My clothes smell. My personal hygiene is not well. I have
been dumpster diving, looking, for cans to sell.

The first light of morning. My belly yearns for food to eat, my eyes still asleep. My brain sends a message to my lips, to shout out a call, for alcohol.

Living out of a whiskey bottle, my life has been torn with sorrow. I am afraid to give it another chance, holding on to a beer can.

My mind has sink to an all time low. I'm reluctant to let it go. Before I can find a bed, my feet will lead me to a place to tread. For money, my hand must beg.

I tried to live my life without a drink, but my mind refuse to think.

On a cold night, I have a terrible time sleeping. When the morning awake, I discover that my eyes have been weeping.

I beg for money, but will accept bread instead, and a roof over my head.

When the rain comes, I seek shelter inside a doorway, or beneath the freeway. For the safety of a room, I have no money to pay.

I feel as though a flame burns inside of me. Firing up the coals, deep in my soul. Keeping my feet moving up, and down a lonesome road.

My mind struggles to think. My eyes starts to weep. My lips craves another drink, more than food to eat.

I smoke cigarettes, when I can find them. I cough a lot, right on the spot.

At times, my body has no feeling. My eyes roll back into my head, staring at the ceiling.
Grasping for lost thoughts, as my thought pattern, is brought to a halt.

In the corners of the street. Nickels and dimes, I try to find. Unsteady on my feet; my health has swiftly declined.

The game of life, I didn't play well. lost between hard times; living in a drunken spell. Nothing on my mind; reading unkind signs.

A time to rise; a time to fall. No time to pause. Angels from heaven, watches over the lost, with eyes of all.

ROMANCE BY NIGHT

Romance by Night; kisses
  Before the twilight. Stars
    Take to the air. Shades of
      Darkness, and love affairs.

    Blazing infatuation; loving
      Sensations. Embracing the
        Eyes of dawn, romancing
          Till the morning sun.

Flames giving sight. Tender
  Arms hold you tight. Engulfed
    By softness of charm. Fire and light,
      Sweethearts burning up the night.

    Romance by Night, hearts
      Filled with delight. Gentle
        Love will bloom. Beneath
          The ocean moon.

Moonlight rays, reflecting off
  the waterways. Across the blue
    lakes, caressing lovers come
      together, before the dawn awakes.

    Dreamy music slices the air.
      Romantic lyrics everywhere.
        Embracing the night, that
          Young hearts shares.

Romance by Night. Ships
    Sails with lovers amid the
        Harbor lights. A toast, riding
            The wind across the seacoast.

    Love songs laces the air,
        Sweethearts dances in pairs.
        Awaiting the light of the moon.
            Humming a tune, it will come soon.

    Romance by Night

A DIAMOND RING

I give to you a diamond ring,
    with a shine that sing.
        A diamond adorned in the
            finest gold, the pattern
                of a unique mold.

A diamond ring, I present
    to you. Accompanied
            by a golden
                necklace too.

A precious stone, set in gold.
    That sparkles a bright,
            that eyes
                may behold.

A ring, a necklace, I bring.
    With a wish that
            love won't
                be rejected.

A ring of beautiful dreams,
    that's untold. Blossoms
            of love that
                will unfold.

It holds the magic of true love,
 that has been captured
    from the brightest
     stars above.

A gift from the sea. Reflecting
 glitter for the way
    your life will
     always be.
It holds a piece of the ocean.
 Casting brilliant colors
    of true
     emotions.

A lovely diamond ring. Like
 wings that takes to the sky.
    A heavenly treasure
    before my eyes.

STIRRING THE SANDS
OF ROMANCE

Stirring the sands of romance. That glitters from the
sunny waves.
Than washes away,
On rainy
Days.

New love sparkles in the harbor lights. Blinded by the
darkness
Of night. Times
Of laughter,
Left in the
Sands.

Tear drops, that falls from a faded romance. The colors
of
Delight, flickers
Across the
Twilight.

Where romance can bring a beautiful sight. Then is
lost in
The night. The sky may
Be a lovely blue,
But the sands
Of romance
Can turn
Against
You.

True love took a pause, then romance was lost. No one
could
Understand. The stolen
Romance, that was
Barely protruding
From the
Sands.

Stirring the sands of romance. Beneath the summer
showers,
And dying flowers. Untold
Truth remains, that
Ruby lips try to
Explain.

Bells that ring, birds that sing, lovers that swing. Days
that
Were once fair,
Now lost in
The sun
Glare.

Fading love affairs, gone with cascading air. Rhythm
and rhyme,
In the sands of time.
Kind hearts,
Torn apart.

Gunplay, of another day. Scheming for money to pay.
Seeking
Romance, that
Has faded
Away.

Blue skies, and sunny smiles. Music that soothe the air.
Love
Once was everywhere.
In the sands of
Romance, life
Can be just
A dance.

Like warm flames that went with the winds. Stirring
the sands
Of romance, that
May someday
come to an
End.

Stirring the Sands of Romance

LOVING YOU THROUGH
ALL SEASONS

Loving you through all seasons. Beneath the full moon.
    loving you through
        all seasons. When
            true love is in full
                bloom.

In spring, when the weather is mild. Where the brightest
    stars shine. Giving
        a glow to the warm
            night sky.

When the early sunrise of summer, bring the beginning
    of warm summer days.
        where the rays of sunlight
           put a smile upon your
                face.

    Loving you through
        all seasons,
            for the perfect
                reasons.

Beneath the summer showers. Beams the rainbow flowers.
    spinning with an
        array of loveliness.
            through the winter
                hours.

Through the season of summer. During the mystic twilight.
  loving you
        Forever, with
              the stars of
                    night.

Loving you through all seasons. As a gentle spring. When
  flowers bloom, and
        humming birds sang.
              such a lovely season,
                    with the joy it
                          bring.

When summer passes into fall. The sun, and rain remains. Then
  comes the fog.
        For The seasons
              of you. I love
                    them all.

  When winter give
        way to spring.
              you make my
                    heart sang.

Loving you through the season of autumn. When the green
  trees, trade color with
        The leaves. When the
              winter winds come
              calling. As the leaves
                    go falling.

Despite the winter chill. Sweet love for you, my heart will always
feel. During the winter
snowfall. My ears
can hear the season's
Love call.

Loving you through the season of winter, across the icy lakes.
When we dance
beneath the falling
snowflakes.

When the winter storms came. Unleashing a cascade of rain.
Loving you through
the winter winds.
beyond the season's
end.

A CRUSH ON YOU

In the way my eyes gaze
  Upon you. Beneath the
    Skies of blue. I thought
      You knew.
      I have a crush on you.

Each moment we share.
  If only for a spell. When
    Days are made anew.

      I have a crush on you.

When the gentle flowers
 Gives blossoms to spring.
 I hear music in the air. As you
 Make my heart sang. With lyrics
      Of love too.
      I have a crush on you.

If you could only touch my
 Lips, with a tender kiss. Forever
 In a day, I insist. My love for you
    Will pierce the winds, with a heart
      Of gold that bears no end.

  Each day my love will
    Blossom anew, and
    Flourish as the springtime
      Skies a blue.
      I have a crush on you.

WISHING A DAYDREAM

Wishing a daydream
true. That bring true
love to someone
like you.

Wishing my dark
sky to yield blue,
and bring back
sunny days. Like the
smile on your face,
so gently do.

Wishing a daydream
true. That grows our
heart with joy and
laughter, and bring
a rainbow of color
for the both of us.

With tender hearts
that are filled with
love and trust.

Wishing a daydream
true. When we lie
beneath satin sheets.
Where tears are
forbidden to fall.
laced with cheer,
and no time to weep.

Wishing a daydream
true. As thoughts races
through my mind, as
I daydream of you.

Wishing that you
have bright
daydreams too.

Wishing daydreams,
that fly with the
Winds, and rises with
the sun. When I'm
lost in the shadows
of thought, thinking
of us as one.

In a maze of
Daydreams, as I gaze
across the green
meadow. Where
The warm sun beam.

Into my eyes it
will be pleasing.
Into a daydream
on a sunny evening.

Sweet daydreams
looms in my
imagination. As
I stare into the
faraway sky, in
a daydream, I
can see the
Beauty in your eyes.

SHE WORE
BLUE JEANS

She wore blue jeans. When she walked by
in a stride,
she caught
my eye.

Her blue jeans, could be fit for a queen.
When she turned
I could plainly
see, that she
was fancy
free.

My eyes could see that she had a lovely face,
a beautiful babe.
Her skin was
smooth as cream,
as she wore
her blue
Jeans.

As she stood and waited, my mind was
captivated. I could
not take my eyes
of her, for a minute,
or a few. From
behind I got a
fantastic
view.

As far as I was concern, my mind
was wondering
if she like
to have
fun.

I wondered what she would say, if I
ask her out on
a date, or if
it was to
late.

Where did she go? I guess I will never
Know. The way
she wore her
blue jeans, was
like none my eyes,
had ever
seen.

HIT MAN

Hit man! A man without a name. He plays no game. Out
of the night he came, bearing the blame. A path to death,
for money and gold he will lay claim.

My name is Trent. On the streets I was known as Front Leg.
That's because I was lead man in an underground club, run
by thieves and thugs.

I had been involved in crime since I was very young. Living
a life of highs and lows, like a song.
I joined an organization known as the IBT. "The
International Brotherhood of Thieves."

We robbed diamond stores, and jewelry shops. To gain
entrance we would pick the locks. Other times we would
scale the walls, and go in from the top.

Any time during night or day. We would burst a cap in
anyone who tried to block our way.

We robbed armor cars, that carried gold bars. We hit the ones
that would transport huge amounts of money. Whether at
night, or when the days were sunny.

At times it seemed to be exciting. I was torn between fear,
and desire, known as the outlaw's high.

Living a life in the darkness of the underworld, where there
were plenty of loose girls. I was hooked. To get the job
done, I would do whatever it took.

We robbed banks, and jacked cars. Time and time again, men of the IBT would end up behind prison bars.

As time went by. Too, many men I watched die. Then in due time, I had a change of mind. No doubt, I wanted out.

My eyes had seen too, many killings. Too, much stealing, and bloodshed. Men right before my eyes, had fallen, and died.

I took a wife. Tried to live a good life. Got married to a beautiful woman. She didn't like the job I was doing, or the bloodshed, and killings. Nor, the life style I was living.

She ask me to stop. I agreed. One last job I would do. My heart was fill with greed. I felt a burning need for wealth. That's just the way my heart felt.

A selfish notion, that would enlarge my portion. When the last job was done, I would take money right off the top, then the illegal jobs, I would stop.

The IBT was divided into four groups. The South Bens, the North Wings, the East Boys, and the West Angels.

I was the leader of the West Angels. We were fearsome. If anyone hung around us, their lives were in danger. Whether an acquaintance, or a strange.

I would take money from the haul; hide it away, for a later day. I thought that no one would ever know. Before I could pack up and go.

The head of the organization was living large. His name was Al Franco. He was the man who knew how to run the show.

When attending, a gathering that was held twice a year. I saw Al Franco, kill one of the IBT members, with a gunshot to the back of the head. Because one hundred dollars, he had withheld. As a result, his body fell.

There, the South Ben member laid dead. Al Franco, refused to allow for his body to be buried, but burned it instead.

I finally quit the organization. I put away my guns, and stopped cold. We hit the road, myself and my wife. Everything seemed to be moving along, smooth and nice.

We were in route to Chicago. The illegal tasks that I once performed, I refused to do anymore. My wife asked me to stop. Now, it was time to go.

I had took huge amounts of money, right from the top. Thinking that no one would ever know, about the money, and goods. Especially, Al Franco.

We moved into a place in Chicago. Immediately, I got a call, from the boss, Al Franco. He wanted the money back that I had stole, this is what I was told.

He lived the life of a cold bloody crook. Deep in his eyes, lain a killer's look. The evil ways in which he used me, I refused to return the money.

It was a trend. Al Franco, took most of the money that we brought in. For the work I had done, I was granted very little funds. At times I received none.

Later that night, I looked outside my windowpane. I gazed upon someone standing beneath the streetlights. He was a tall strange man, for me, he had came.

He wore a black hat, and a long black trench coat. I realized that beneath his long coat, a gun he would tote.

He started to walk toward the house, with his hands buried in his pockets. It appeared a gun he was cocking.

Right away, my conscious led me to know, this man was working for Al Franco. He was a hit man. With guns in both hands.

He pounded on the front door. "Open up, Front Leg!", is what he said. "Who are you?", I replied. I cracked open the door. Stared into his eyes.

"Come on out!", he yelled. I turned to take cover, but tripped and fell. One hard smash, to the front glass, he burst into the house very fast. I turned to run, scoping for my gun.

Right away, he started spraying the living room with rounds of lead. I yelled to my wife, to take cover beneath the bed.

The debris that splattered off the wall, was flying everywhere. I managed to make my way to a bedroom, and grabbed my 357 magnum. I stood quietly. Waiting to get off rounds. Before my wife comes down.

My eyes could see him walking backward, through the living room, toward the hall.
Moving in closer, with guns ready for kill. I could see that he stood tall. My heart was drenched in fear.

Swiftly, I stepped out into the hall, and pulled the trigger. "Bang! Bang! Bang!" Smoke billowed from my gun. I was not about to run.

Three bullets in his head, his blood splattered across the walls. There, the hit man fell dead.

The elusiveness of my mind, led me to know, more hit men would be sent by Al Franco. For, my protection, I would carry a gun wherever I go.

Before long, I moved from Chicago. Brought my wife along, and found a place of our own, in old Baltimore.

It was a warm summer night, the moon was shinning bright. The stars aligned themselves for a magnificent sight.

I was driving on a road along the countryside. The night was quiet. The stars flickered across the sky. Little did I know, that on this night. I would be in a fight, for my life.

Suddenly, a car came fast from behind, and then bright lights glared into my eyes. I made a motion for it to pass by. Instead the car rammed me from the side.

I sped up, and tried to get away, but before I could go, my conscious led me to know, that this was another hit man, working for, Al Franco.

Out of another day, he was sent to take my life away. Into high speed, my car sped.
Trailing right on my tail, the hit man wanted me dead.

My windshield was hit by a tree limb, I could not lose him, then he rammed my car from behind. My wheels began to squeak, and started to grind.

The tires were smoking up the road, I lost control.
My vehicle landed at the bottom of a ditch. A deep embankment I barely missed. I was in a survival mode.

I grabbed my gun, and began to run. Into the woods, I fled.
The hit man followed, firing rounds of hot lead.

I stopped, and returned fire. "Bang! Bang! Bang! Bang!"
Flames flashed from the barrel of my gun. Gun smoke raised into the air. a bullet struck him in the chest, from my 357 magnum, what an awful mess! The hit man bled. Stretched across the cold ground. He laid dead.

I was exhausted. My mind was in disarray. I had survived another bloody day.

These attempts on my life would have to stop. I would now, have to go, after Al Franco. Keeping it on a down low.

I knew, if I procrastinated, the hit men would have kept on coming. Like thieves in the night, in an attempt to take my life.

I traveled back to my home state, in search of Al Franco. I could not take this kind of drama anymore. It seem to follow me wherever I go.

I paid someone to lure him out into the open. Like a wild animal, that is lured by the smell of fresh meat, into a field, for kill.

It was past midnight. I was ready for a hard fight. The night was chilled, and the winds were still.

Al Franco, was lured by the ever present thought, that he could turn a five hundred thousand dollar deal into millions. No matter whom he had to kill.

His mother, his brother, or whomever got in his way. Their blood he would spill.

I kept my mind keen, as I watched him arrive on the scene. He wore a thousand dollar suit, diamond rings on his fingers. If anything goes wrong, he would not prolong. Only to pull his gun, and begin to shoot.

I called out his name, "Al Franco!" "Who is that?" He replied. "Is that you Front Leg?" He asked. "Yeah, It is me!" I replied. "Did you come back to die?" He asked. I moved in closer. I could see the killer's stare in his eyes.

"What are you doing back in town? Front Leg. By now, I thought you would be dead". "Not yet, Al Franco. That is why I came to see you. I am not dead, and I am not afraid!"

He quickly pulled his gun, and got off three shots. "Bang! Bang! Bang!" A smoking gun, for cover, I turned to run.

He hit me in my right side, as I started to turn. I could feel the burning pain. Then my side went numb.

Before I could pull my gun. Al Franco, stood over me, with his gun aimed for my head. I knew right then and there, I was as good as dead.

Suddenly! Up from behind I heard two shots ring out. "Bang! Bang!" A flash of gun light, in the night. Right before my eyes, I got a big surprise. Al Franco, took two slugs in the back. He spun around, and dropped to the ground. Bleeding and dead, there he could be found.

Doomed to the tomb. For him, life held no more room. By my surprise, my wife had pumped two slugs into his back.

She had saved my life with a vicious attack. Not giving him a chance to shoot back.

Life in prison is what I got. I took the blame for the man my wife shot.

She is living with another man, spending money that I made. I eluded the law for years, burning up my young days.

She is living with a smile on her face, and spending money in uncontrollable ways.

Behind prison walls, my life is at a loss. Doing hard time, for a life of crime.

If I could do it all over again, I would go to school, and live by the golden rules. For me, it is now, to late. I have been a fool. When I thought, I was cool.

FLOATING
BUTTERFLY

Floating butterfly,
flying with ease.
Her wings
across a light
breeze.

Her beautiful colors
adorns the wind,
with quietness
that lie
within.

Taken from flowers
aligning exotic
places. Like
lilies, violets
and daisies.

Floating butterfly,
a gift to the world.
Like diamonds,
and pearls.

A wonderful treasure,
creating a
scenery of
pleasure.

Fluctuating in thin air,
so pretty and fair.
Her beauty cannot
be compared.

Floating in the warmth
of the sunshine.
Blending with
the beauty of
springtime.

A delicate display,
flickering along
the way.

Astride the stillness
of day. Into the
lovely month
of may.

Beneath the blue sky.
Dancing with
beauty as
she fly.

Wearing the colors of
the rainbow, across
the hilltops,
whence she
will go.

As if gliding on ice, with
wings out of paradise.
Floating on air,
beyond the
sun glare.

Floating Butterfly

CHASED BY THE
GHOST OF LOVE

I was entranced. My mind wondered whether my heart
should
take a chance. I was
under her spell.
For her, my heart
had fell. Her words
rendered a
good-bye.

Then, my love for her would die. Blown by the mystic
wind.
Fading into
the night
sky.

A look into her eyes. Revealed that the love, that once lived
in my heart.
Struggled
to come
alive.

My feet began to run away. Evading the past, racing into the
distant day. Chased
by the ghost of
love. Grasping
for ways to
survive.

I could see pale colors looming, from the corner of my eyes.
I could hear the
sound of her
soft voice.
whispering
in the
wind.

From the places whence she had been. Speaking tender
words
that my ears
had once
heard.

My heart was afraid. Into the cold wind, my person took
Flight, and fled.
In hope that my
heart would never
be broken
again.

Chase by the ghost of love. When the fierce wind blow. Back
into the past,
my heart
refused to
go.

My feet ran fast. The ghost of love followed with the key,
to unlock the
past.

Haunting memories lingered in my mind, of a dying love
that could never
last. Cut from
the ends of
time.

My heart had been cheerful. Chased by the ghost of love,
with a heart of
darkness. My
mind was
fearful.

My feet ran faster as it came. My heart was racked by pain.
Running through
city streets,
where love
was said, to
be dead.

Chased by the ghost of love. Carrying spirits of broken
hearts.
Carrying fading
memories of
romantic
pages, ripped
apart.

Haunting the inward parts of my soul, for love revising.
Chased by the
ghost of love.
When the low
moon was
rising.

WHEN MY HEART
WAS CRUEL

I have been a fool. When I knew
The rules. Yet I let you go.
When my heart
Was cruel.

I regret the day when you waltz
Through the door. We had
Our final dance, and
My eyes would
See you no
More.

Left behind on the edge of
Yesterday. I can still
Hear the sweet
Words you use
To say.

I have tried to search for new love,
But my heart refused to go. I
Could never find another
Like you. I remember
The time, when you
Told me so.

My days have no sunshine. The
Stars have disappeared
From my
Nights.

My heart is drenched in the dark
Water of pain. Up against the
Fading shadows of life,
I can never be
The same.
It was you, I clearly deceived.
I should have known that
You would not
Be at ease.

My intentions were good, but
I was misunderstood.
I have been a fool.
When my heart
Was cruel.

ATTACK DOGS

Attack dogs, who will be the next to fall? A news flash, from the city of Silver Nash. A man brutality killed by three vicious dogs. His body badly torn. Found laying on his lawn.

They crouched behind tall grass. Moving in extremely fast, ripping the man's body very bad. A red faded pickup truck was noticed leaving the scene, where the dog attack was bloody, and mean.

News bulletin, from Clear Waters, a small town. A woman was found, laying dead beneath a clothesline.

Eye witnesses reported seeing three huge dogs coming from the yard. The woman's body seemed to be torn apart.

It was reported that the dogs were covered in blood, at the time the attack occurred.

Two other persons had been brutality attacked, by three vicious dogs, during the morning of heavy fog. The area appeared to be deserted. It had been clearly reported.

The evening sun was slowly moving across town, leaving a trail, for the shade of sundown, when I notice three dogs, coming down Wind Dell road.

It was a chilly day. The air was cold, the wind was blowing up dust, and leaves along the way.

The three dogs were very large. One appeared to be scarred. Their gigantic feet were pounding the ground. Their mouths made growling sounds, as they moved their large heads up and down.

Their brown, and reddish hairy coats, were dirty. After they came closer, I could see that they were sweaty, and bloody.

People in the neighborhood referred to them as, The Attack Dogs. They were aware of persons who had been brutalized, by the huge dogs, as time went by.

They were followed closely, by a slow moving faded pickup truck.

I stood in the front yard, as the dogs came. I tried to hide, but I watched them, from the corner of my eyes.

They appeared to be tired. Their tongues were visible outside of their mouths, hanging long, flapping from side to side, as they passed me by.

The pickup truck came to a stop, directly in front of me. It back fired, making a loud pop. It was driven by a man we called, "Crazy Willey."

We called him that, because of the rude, and violent behavior, he displayed. At times, when he went passed our place.

He lived along, deep in the back woods, at the edge of Wind Dell road. From behind the trees, his mailbox barely showed.

He refused to shave. Small eye glasses he wore on his face. His belly protruded outward from beneath his overalls, liken to that of Santa Claus.

He drove his pickup truck, closely in front of me. Then, he parked; the engine continue to run. Making a low squeaky hum.

"Hey boy! Where is your Pappy?" He asked. "He's not here," I replied. He projected a cold deep stare into my eyes. I stared right back into his face. The manor in which he approached me, seemed to be out of place.

"Well, when you lay eyes on him, tell him I know he slept with my wife, at least once or twice. Before she went away, on new year's day."

"My dad did not sleep with your wife! Not even once or twice, before she left," I replied. As I tried to contain myself.

The huge dogs turned around, storming toward me. Pounding the ground. I assumed, I was about to go down. I trembled in fear. Their ears were set for a kill.

I stood still. They came near me in an attack mode, showing their long yellow teeth. Clawing at the road, with their big feet. It occurred to me, that I may soon be dead meat.

"Well boy! It might be time, for you, and your Pappy to die," said Crazy Willey, as he wore a deceitful smile. He whistled at the dogs. In what seemed to be, a dog's call. They moved away, headed into the day.

I quickly turned toward the house, and ran inside.
I was appalled. He wasn't listening to what I had to say at all.

I told my sisters and brothers, what Crazy Willey had said. My mother was listening, and became afraid.

As a boy, I was stubborn, and refused to be intimidated. I was not going to let Crazy Willey, and his dogs, get away with what he had done.   I was going to send them on the run.

My family owned three dogs. They were kept inside a pin, in the back yard. They were mean and hard.

Crazy Willey, owned trained fighting dogs. They had been fighting in the underworld about one year. One had lost his ear.

I went to my cousins house. They lived a little ways, up the street from us. They brought out their hunting dogs. They seemed to be rough and tough.

Altogether, we had six dogs ready to rumble. They were ready to get down and dirty, on the ground, before sundown.

We marched down Wind Dell road, the day was chilly and cold. The dogs were on the move, steam billowed from their nose. They were bucking for a fight, before the night.

We approached Crazy Willey's house, that sat near the end of Wind Dell road. When the day was cold.

It was overrun by trees, tall grass, and weeds. Butterflies, and bumblebees, fluttered among the leaves.

The Attack Dogs, were a few feet apart, standing in the front yard, in their attack mode. They began moving out into the road, growling and exposing their sharp teeth, ready to unload.

All of a sudden, like a pack of wild wolves, they attack. Using speed that kills, with fighting dog skills. Our dogs fought back, but seemed to be over matched.

They went for the throats, our dogs were being choked. Two of our dogs stood their ground. Fighting hard, right from the start, refusing to go down.

Dust was flying everywhere. Fur and hair, were in the air. Blood was dripping to the ground. It was a bloody scene, vicious and mean.

A couple of our dogs had been beat down, Stretched across the ground.

It was a horrible sight. Our dogs fought hard, with all their might. Suddenly, Crazy Willey, bailed out of the house, with a shotgun, blasting shots into the air. Madness, and obscene language proceeded out of his mouth.

He fired twice, bringing a halt to the fight. breaking the dogs apart, calling the Attack Dogs back into the yard.

He threaten to kill all of us. We had, had enough. Our dogs were injured and bloody.

By the mixture of sweat, blood, and dirt. The area had become muddy.

One of my cousins started to cry. He thought our dogs were going to die.

We slowly moved along, with our dogs barely hanging on. We hand carried one of them back home, but he didn't last long.

Early the next morning, we buried him, and covered the grave with rocks, and tree limbs.
To keep the vultures away, so they, would not eat him for prey.

A few day had passed. Then, early one chilly Saturday morning. My dad, brother, and I, were out hunting on the eastside of Hollow Lake. Deep in the back woods, near the edge of Wind Dell road. The day was frozen cold.

We were hunting deer, near an open field, waiting for some to appear.

It began to snow. It had snowed the night before. Suddenly,
We could hear dogs barking, coming in our direction. We
move into the weeds, and hid behind the trees, for our
protection.

It was the three Attack Dogs, as they chased a deer, across
the open field. Running through the snow, the deer was on
the go.

I fired a shot into the air. The dogs retreated, moved out,
and took another route. Back into the falling snow, they
would go.

 I could barely see Crazy Willey, standing outside,
near his faded pick up truck.
The back tires were buried in the mud below. He seemed to
be very stuck, and couldn't get it to go.

The snow was heavily falling, the Attack Dogs, he was
calling.

He was armed with a long double barrel shotgun, pointing
toward the sky. A handgun was hanging from his side. I
kept a keen eye.

In an instant, he let out a yell! "Who wants to die first?"
He began to curse, speaking bold words, when the matter
occurred.

"Attack Dogs!", he yelled. Out of nowhere! The three
huge dogs were storming straight toward us. Unleashing
lightning strikes, of attacks.

My brother turned to run, but he stumbled and fell. Their ears were pinned back. Their wet tongues were hanging out of their mouths. The day turned bad, as they moved in fast, ready for the kill. On that very day, our blood would be spilled.

There was no time to think. My mind went blank. The dogs were wild and unruly, they displayed it truly. My dad told me to run, as he raised his gun.

The three dogs were upon us in a flash, with a vicious attack.

My dad was knocked down, to the ground, the dogs bellowed a horrible sound.

My brother tried to go for his gun. One of the dogs grabbed his leg in a terrible attack. Ripping his leg; climbing up his back. He cried out in pain, as he struggled to loosen himself, when the dogs came.
My dad was being torn apart. To free him from the jaws, of the Attack Dogs, I tried very hard. I struggled to get them to release my dad, right from the start.

I managed to grab my gun, then fired twice. "Bang! Bang!" The shots rang out. The Attack Dogs scattered about.

Running away, into the frozen day. I aimed over their heads, they turned, and fled.

Crazy Willey, came running toward me shooting to kill. My blood he wanted to spill, with hatred, his heart was filled.

"Bang! Bang! Bang!!!." I could see the flames, flashing from his gun. He had gone insane.

I went down, I had took two round, in my leg. I could feel the hot lead burning beneath my skin. I dragged myself across the cold ground, into the woods, trying not to get hit again.

I could barely see Crazy Willey, storming toward me, through the falling snow, with his gun blazing. I had no place to go.

I returned fire, dropping him to the ground, with lightning rounds. Blood began to flow, dripping into the cold snow.

Gun smoke, entered my eyes. I felt as though I wanted to cry, I could not let my dad, and brother die. I struggled to stay alive.

I had a court hearing. I was tried, for killing Willey. My heart was fill with pity. I was exonerated, for killing a man in self-defense. A deed, the law did not go against.

It was a horrible time. I try to erase it from the walls of my mind. At the end of the day, it is still hard to unwind. Bad dreams rises from my memory, all the time.

Deep down inside, I still feel responsible, for the way I handled the situation. I realize, that I could have died, and that life is not a game. Nevertheless, by killing a man. My life will never be the same.

Attack Dogs

SIPPING TEA

Sipping tea, just you
and me. That can
unlock a broken
heart, with
a magic
key.

Where the evening
brings fresh air,
and the soft
winds that
blows upon
your hair.

Sipping tea, beneath
the evergreen tree.
Sweeten with
your love,
that only
my eyes
can see.

Beneath the light
of the moon.
A place where
our love can
bloom.

Where the song
birds of our
happiness, can
sing a new
tune.

Sipping tea, In love
are we. Holding
hands, when
there is no
plan.

A flicker in the
moment, that
only our hearts
can understand.

Wishes to come
true, for things
we long
to do.

Together we dance,
a stroll in the
sand.

A diamond ring,
for your heart
to sing.

Sipping tea, we can
always be. One
beating heart,
never to be
Apart.

EYES IN THE SKY

Eyes in the sky, watching from a distant
high. Lurking in the
night, looking
in secret
sites.

Watching every move you make, every chance
you take. Wherever you
Roam, in places
you don't
belong.

Eyes in the sky. Hypnotized, nothing can
get by. lurking in the
Wind, in places
where your
lover has
been.

No time for sleeping, watching whose creeping.
Eyes in the sky, sees red,
when you tell lies.
Highlighting
the truth,
you can't
deny.

Peering in far off places, seeing new faces.
Prying eyes, on the
rise. Looking at you,
zooming in on all
the things
you
do.
Hiding from the light, sweeping across the night.
Eyes in the sky, never shy.
Watching those who
never cry. Those
who chose to
roam. Those
who don't
belong.

Eyes in the Sky.

LADY SUPREME

Here she comes again. A lady supreme.
with those bright beautiful eyes.
That sparkle rays from the
sunglow, with a bit
of surprise.

Here she comes, with a wiggle in her
walk, and a voice of loveliness
when she talk. A sexy smile,
that drives men
wild.

When I hear her name. I get
a thrill of excitement,
that I can't
contain.

When I see her face. I'm intrigued,
by her radiant beauty
that light up my
dark days.

She is the one, and only. The love
of a dream, the lady of joy.
A picture of sunshine,
a Lady Supreme.
A Beauty
Queen.

FACES IN THE WIND

Faces in the wind. Memories
of long familiar
friends,

and all the delightful
places that we
have been.

Thoughts that races.
Reminiscence of
summertime
places,

of guys and gals,
when laughter
filled the
air.

Faces in the wind. Of class
mates, and faded dates.
Young hearts, of love
that would never
depart.

Those girlfriends, and
boyfriends, whose
kisses set
A trend.

Later to discover, that
they may have
been, the
next of
kin.

Fieldtrips and picnics.
Sunny days when
classes would
mix.

Homecomings, and
the games we
played. New
jokes we
would
trade.

Stars in the night,
gave us a
familiar
sight.

Putting on a spectacular
show. Mirroring the
places where
we use
to go.

Faces in the wind. With
memories that
will never
end.

YOU MUST BE FALLING
IN LOVE

You must be falling in love.
  As the brightest stars falls from
  The dark sky above. Radiating soft
      Starlight that gleams in your eyes.

      Illuminating a brighter sparkle
          To your smile. In the height of
          Summer days. Sunny rays adds
              A radiant gloss to your face.

              You must be falling in love.

A sweet song your heart has
    Been singing. Your feet started
    To dance when no music was
        Playing. The new joy that I see

        In your eyes. A face filled with surprise.
        Assuming, that in your heart new
        love is blooming. The way you wear
            your hair, suggest that you are
                approaching a new love affair.

                You must be falling in love.

The style in which you dance.
    Infer an arrival of new romance.
    In your heart new love will be concealed.
        The sparkle in your smile reveals, the
           Awakening love that you feel.

           You must be falling in love.

THE JUNGLE OF HELL

Into the Jungle of Hell, he fell. A man named, "Nate Morell." He was the baddest man to ever walk the face of earth. Every man he met, he would curse.
He would cheat, lie, and steal. Men he didn't like, he would kill.

Thrust into the Jungle of Hell, chained and shackled from head to feet. Human food, no more, would he eat.

He awaken from a long sleep, to a big surprise, staring Satan, straight into his eyes. Among scorpions and snakes, near a burning lake.

Where love is dead, and hate is alive, instead. Where the lost souls toil, for days, and there is no resting place.

The face of Satan wore deep frowns. The end of his long tail dragged across the hot coals, that aligned the hell grounds.

Two curved horns extended from each side of his head, with eyes that were fiery red. His head was divided into, two parts, with a body that's stone hard.

Satan took Morell, by his chains, and showed him the place in the Jungle of Hell, where he would be staying.

He showed him the lake of fire that burned high, where many souls have died.

Morell thought he could survive, and escape, from the burning lake.

They went pass the fire breathing pit, that was eternally lit.

Nate Morell, had been accused. Hell fire awaited, that could not be diffused.

He would have to pay, for the blood he spilled, and the men he has killed. A wicked mind set, he refused to change. Living in hell, there is nothing to gain.

He tried to run, to a place without fire, but found none. This was the dreadful place, where all the bad men would come. The Jungle of Hell, where many have fell. A lesson he would now learn.

Running through dead trees, that bear no leaves. Through the hot liquid fire, that flows through the gutters of hell, he was propelled.

He looked for a cool drank of water, to quench his thirst, but the water was curst. Wandering around, looking for a cool down.

He fought with the devil hard, and long, but the devil was big, and strong. Morell was beaten, and dragged along. Ash and smoke billowed high, as fallen souls would burn and die.

Before he went to hell. Morell, had been slogging through the brutal swamps. The stars appeared to be falling from the sky, right before the town people eyes. The moon failed to shine, for a period of time.

Chased by the cops, then they got the drop. He had left behind a trail of murders, and aggravated assaults, before he was caught.

He was swung high, before many peering eyes, beneath the angry sky.

Hung from a tall tree, so everyone could see, that Nate Morell, the baddest man on earth, was going to burning hell, for an eternity.

Thrust into the jungle of Hell, to the bottom he fell. He refused to repent, to hell he was sent. Covered in bloodstains, there he would remain.

Where darkness rule over time, and the sun will never shine. Where the moon and stars, have been barred, from bringing light to the underworld. Where souls have been scarred.

Morell, was Shackled and chained, along with another man. An open book, hang on a steel hook. An hourglass, with evidence from the past. As he journeyed toward hell, he left a bloody trail, align with deadly details.

Bad man Nate Morell, was put on trial. His soul was sentence to burn and die. In the Jungle of Hell, where he ran naked, and wild.

Where wild beast galloped through hell fire, looking to devour old souls, that had grown cold.

Where the bad men escaped into burning trees, gasping for air to breathe. Thrust into fiery pits, when the flames were lit.

He looked for a way to escape. Dragons with wings and claws, hurled flames of fire from their gigantic jaws, onto the lost. Fire of hell they would breathe, burning anyone who try to leave.

Wild beasts would eat you alive. No way to survive. They lurked along lifeless trees, waiting for sinful souls, that falls among the burning weeds.

Nate Morell, struggled to find a way to escape. Suddenly, he was loosed. His soul, he stole, and made way back to earth, when the night was cold.

His body had grown wrinkled and old. A ghost, he resembled the most.

At the gates of hell, the devil was awaiting the return of Nate Morell, with a hell fork in hand, fire in his eyes, and demons by his side. Itching for Morell's soul, to be thrust into a hell hole.

Where fresh air has been denied, from bringing a cool spell, to the jungle of Hell.

Where the wind has been brought to an end, forbidden to ever return again.

Before long. The devil called for his soul searcher, to capture Nate Morell, and bring him back to hell.

The soul searcher appeared beneath the black sky. The darken moon was hanging high, the fading stars seemed to hide. With a strike of lightning, his eyes were frightening.

Long black hair covered his body. He walked upright on two hind legs.

Out of his huge mouth, hung his long reddish tongue, lapped across his sharp pointed fangs.
He ran with powerful legs into the wind.

He was a "Werewolf." Out of the darkness of hell, he was propelled. Running in haste, time he didn't waste.

He was on the trail, of Nate morell. The man who had stole his soul, and escaped from hell, from the fiery lake, scorpions and snakes.

The night was cold and dark. You could hear the raging wolves howl, and the mad dogs bark.

The Werewolf mission was to capture bad man Nate Morell, find his tracks, and bring him back, to hell.

The winds blew fierce. The Werewolf sprinted through the city streets, and across the fields.

Stormy weather was stirring, the appearance of the Werewolf sent the town people fearing.

Hard winds blew, the Werewolf would vigorously pursue. On the trail of Nate Morell, who escaped from burning hell. Running in the wind, drunken with sin.

He ran across the expressway, in the light of day. Through the parks, and boulevards, when it was dark. Through the city streets, in a town that never sleep.

He ran in the heart of darkness, away from the light, into the night. The town people were thrust into fright.

The Werewolf was trailing, the twilight, had been failing. Fiery red foam proceeded from his mouth, emblazing the night.

Bad man Nate Morell, wandered beneath the dark shadows of the moonlight. Lurking around, looking for a cool down.

The low moon was rising. The starlight was revising. The fog had set in, then carried away by a strong wind.

The Werewolf was prowling, in the thickness of the dark woods. You could hear him howling, searching behind trees, and rocks as fast as he could, for Nate Morell, the man who had escaped from hell.

In a full sprint, Nate Morell was running. He knew the Werewolf was coming. At his life's end, he was sent to pay for his sins, in the jungle of Hell. Where Satan rules. Many men he have made fools.

To the bottom of hell, he once fell. Where men cold hearts, have been melted down. None will confess, they will get no rest.

Nevertheless, bad man Nate Morell, had escaped from the Jungle of Hell. Scorched by fire. His face was fiery red, as he fled. It appeared that his body had been cooked in hot coals. wind blew right through his weary soul.

The Werewolf came up from behind, With teeth and claws, he pierced his spine. Nate Morell struggled vigorously to get away, but not on this day. For his sins, he would have to pay.

The Werewolf ripped his soul, right out of his ghostly body, when the weather was cold.

He clinched his claws into his side. Open his mouth wide, and let go of a frightening yell. Bad man Nate Morell ,was thrust into a dead man's spell.

Like a hungry beast, that roams the wild for its prey. The Werewolf from hell, roamed the dark woods, looking for bad man, Nate Morell. He carried his soul, back to the Jungle of Hell, where he fell.

There, he will remain, living in burning flames. Refused to repent, to hell, his soul was sent.

EYES OF
DANGER

Eyes of Danger. She grew up living among total strangers. Going by the name of, "Green Eyes." Known as the wild child.

She considers herself a grand prize. Living with a wanted man, spending time with another, when ever she got the chance.

A touch of cheer, with eyes to kill, she revealed. A kiss for a thrill, looking for the money of another. A heart beating with trouble.

Men have died, for a kiss from the woman called, "Green Eyes," and from the tails she told, with a deadly smile.

Into the night, she would go out. Strolling about. A trade for the street life, in view of a hefty price. A trend, beneath her skin. An old familiar sin, that packs a powerful end.

Eyes of Danger. Reminiscence of a fallen angel. A pleasure to look upon. Her hair was fair and long. The beauty in her face was on display, with features that would melt your heart away.

The look of a queen, her eyes revealed a shade of green.

Her ruby lips were sweet as apple pie. Her heart went bearing lies.

Roaming the streets, in search of a treat, looking for items to steal. Jacking cars, and other automobiles.

She was born the daughter to a harlot. She grew up as a little girl, living her life in an uncertain world.

She seemed to be shy, by the look in her eyes. However, she was sly, considered herself a grand prize.

Green Eyes, failed to see, that her life was outside the rim of reality.

Her heart was cold as steel. Bearing no fear, never shedding a tear. Others have cry, for the sake of Green eyes.

Raised by a woman, who operated a gambling house. Where men would go to seek female pleasure. Take chances on winning a small treasure.

Rolling in the fast lanes; cold blood running through her veins, clenching guns in both hands.

Running with the wrong men. She didn't think twice, when wielding a knife.

The madness in her eyes was a code of silence. She participated in gang violence.

Eyes of Danger. A child among strangers. The beauty in her face, men would praise.

The gentleness in her arms, was of a deadly charm. With tendencies to deceive, and tricks up her sleeve.

To the street life, she was sold. In a different mode, she would lose control. Speaking words that was mean, and bold.

Eyes of Danger, with a smile of an angel. A kiss of death, caught up in a love fest, someone will be laid to rest.

Beware of the black widow, that crawls upon your pillow. With a poisonous bit. She will eat her mate, and seal his fate, then fad into the night.

Green Eyes, running wild, with guns by her side. Listening to hip-hop, around the clock, pushing buttons never wanting to stop.

Living her life cold, that's the way she rolled. Based upon an in depth probe.

The beauty in her face, disappeared. During her drunken years. Living the street life, with bad advise. Love trading, a body slowly fading.

No more, was she appealing. Packing a gun while robbing and stealing. For human life, she had no feeling.

Green Eyes. Working scams and cons. She was the best. For the love of money, she became obsessed.

She shot a man in the chest. Homicide was the story in the press. A crime of first degree murder, she has confessed. Behind prison walls, she was laid to rest.

Green Eyes. Telling lies, no tears to cry. Never time to apologize.

Eyes Of Danger

STEALING THE NIGHT AWAY

The moon has drifted
    Beyond the dark sky.
    The stars have melted
        Into the light of day.
            Then comes the sun,
        Stealing the night away.

The morning sky cradled
    The birth of dawn. Beckon
    The arrival of the beauty,
        A day will display.
            Here comes the sun,
        Stealing the night away.

The rise of early morning is
    Washed by the falling dew.
    The milky ways ceased to
        Dance or come out to play.
            Then comes the sun,
        Stealing the night away.

The shades of darkness melts
    Into the birth of light. The song
    Birds sang out for the break of
        Day. The shadow of bright colors
            Evaded a delay.
            Here comes the sun,
        Stealing the night away.

Before the start of a summer
   Day. When wild geese awaken
   From winter sleep, and began
      To mate and play.
               Then comes the sun,
         Stealing the night away.

The bright morning clouds
   Flicker across the sky.
   Putting on a dazzling show,
      As in the lovely month of may.
               Here comes the sun,
         Stealing the night away.

THE CREW OF GUNS
AND ROSES

The Crew of Guns and Roses, were men who would do anything, for wealth. Since their childhood, this is the drive, their hearts have felt.

When they were young boys. Roses grew wild, near their homes, for miles. Their parents grew rose gardens that were cherished, and admired, by passer-bys.

Their fathers would come home with money, and other valuable, as pay for their work, and trade. During the boys childhoods day. The money, and valuables were said to be roses.

The boys organized a tree house club, and called it "Guns and Roses." Money they loved. They paid dues, and made rules, that were against the law. Only a dollar sign' their eyes saw. To them life seemed to be cozy, everything appeared to be coming up roses.

When they grew into men, they maintained their membership; upgrading the club, and became a group of sophisticated thugs. Known as the Crew of Guns and Roses. paying the price, with death, or life.

Before they could drive, bikes they would ride. Taking money, goods. Then, they would run and hide. To them the limit was beyond the sky.

The word Roses, became their code, for money and gold.

Anything boosted and sold.

Rolling in a 4 x 4 Hummer, that shined like a full moon, upon the night, rolling beneath the streetlights.

There hearts were cold as ice, their minds, sharp like a knife. With nerves of steel, ready to pull of a heist. Their future lies, in an early graveyard hole. The devil, has a ransom on their souls.

The night was wide awake. Business was buzzing. Everyone played for high stakes. In a city that never sleep. Where a huge amount of money, was yours to keep.

The moon was shining like a neon light, across the black night. Shooting stars were tearing through the sky, fiercely and fast. As if they were trying to escape, before the midnight pass.

The clock struck midnight, there about. The sand in the hour glass drained out.

Suddenly, a loud smashing noise was coming from across town. Making a destructive sound.

The Crew of Guns and Roses, rolled into town, ridding four deep. In their huge Black Hummer. Ready to knock off an all night jewelry store. Looking for a big score.

They slammed their vehicle right into the side wall, front grill, and all. The walls came crashing down, slamming to the ground.

My name is Ziggy. A boy of the crew. We grabbed all the Roses. Including the ATM machine. We took it all, and left the scene, carrying out a systematic scheme.

The jewelry store was turned into a waste. Before the Crew left, We shot up the place, setting it ablaze. We were a wild bunch, living by a hunch.

Gunshots rang out, the sheriffs were running about, firing rounds at the huge Black Hummer, in an attempt to make the Crew pay, as we sped away.

Gunning with a Crew of four. We were on the go, making tracks. Then we fired back. Putting down two Sheriffs. It wasn't a pretty site, blazing up the night. Committing a double homicide, before the day arrived.

Drinking whiskey and wine that showed on our face. Gas fumes raised into a haze.

The Crew of Guns and Roses, gunning for money and gold, power and control. Boys from the hood, misunderstood, running when they could.

The Crew was ripping through city streets, in a quest to get away. Evading the cops, who tried to make them pay.

To the other side of town, we would go. smashing into an all night gambling lounge, about a quarter to four.

Bailing out of the Hummer. We burst in, feeling crazy again. Slammed the doors to keep all the rich folk in. We began pumping killer rounds, telling everyone to get down. Gunning for Roses, That's money and gold, from the all night casinos.

We open fire, blasting rounds into the ceiling. Creating a threatening feeling.
One of the crew boys begin barking out orders.

He was my Brother. His name was Zack, constantly in trouble.

"Alright you high rollers, and money controllers, hear this," he said. "We want all of your Roses."

"Everybody hit the dusty floor. Get down and dirty, and don't turn around, or like a dog, you will be cut down, with my M-16, or an AK-47. Today is not your lucky eleven."

"Everybody empty their pockets. Put all your money, jewelry, and gold in this black sack, and don't hold nothing back."

"Rip off your clothes, and throw them on the floor. Don't turn your heads around, or you will be gunned down," said Zack. "make it fast. Come on, the night is not going to last."

It was midnight madness. The air was filled with fear and sadness. Women were crying and screaming. Across the street from the lounge, the bright lights on the shinny Black Hummer, were beaming.

"Let's get out of here." said Zack. "Come on Ziggy, grab all the Roses. Move it." Swiftly, we bailed out, of the casino.

Two Security guards burst onto the scene, hard and mean, blasting lots of rounds. I could hear the bullets near me, striking the ground.

The Crew fired back. Putting the guards down. We jumped into the Hummer, and begin to speed off. Two lives had been lost.

The cops rolled in. They were yelling, for everybody to stay down. They began to unleash a hail of gun rounds, creating a war zone sound.

Gun smoke billowed into the wind, the Crew was out numbered by ten.

Men trembled with fear. Two Security Guards had been killed.

They came out of the night, ready for a fight. Cut down with an automatic machine gun, laying their bodies down, stretched across the dirty ground.

It was midnight madness. Powerful guns we were blasting. The Crew of Guns and Roses. Gunning, for money and gold. Power and control.

Dogs barked like wolves. Coyotes could be heard crying out across the mountainside. Men had died.

The Crew rolled in with unstoppable firepower. Hails of bullets were flying through the midnight hour.

We blasted our way through police barricades. Scattered across the street, twisted metal, and debris laid.

The powerful Hummer slammed through police cruisers. We were in a hard fight, refusing to be the losers.

Blazes of gunfire we would trade. Gun smoke was carried by the wind, then it began to fad.

Police cruisers were demolished, hot flames burned into the black night.

Reaching high, and glowing bright, cutting into the darkness with burning light.

The Crew sped across the city streets, slamming through traffic. Those who dare to get in our way, their eyes would not see the light of day.

We crashed into police cars, making stops at whiskey bars. Getting intoxicated, drawing up maps of places to rob.

We were a wild bunch, living by a hunch.
The cops gave chase, but were lost across the freeways.

The Crew, gunning for gold, power and control. Talking trash, then away we dash. Criminal minds buried in the darkness of time.

Mask men, no one knew who we were, or where we had been. Out of control, burning up freeways, and country roads.

The crew moved back to the other side of town. A popular nightspot, where the music was loud, and the dancing was hot. With guns in hand, the Crew burst on the scene, insane and mean.

"Stop the music, and nothing will be confusing," hollered my Brother, Zack.

"This is a stickup, we want all your Roses. Everybody take off their clothes. Nothing personal, this is just the way we roll. Give up all your money, jewelry, and gold."

"Hey man, the one behind the table. Do you hear what I'm saying? Do you understand?

Don't be stupid. Don't start nothing, and there won't be nothing."

Some of the club goers were strapped. A gun battle pursued. Three men were killed, giving the Crew a thrill.

At high speed, we raced back across the city, where the light were pretty, in an attempt to confuse the cops, with every stop.

Blowing up building, using hand grenades, racing from place-to-place.

We hit an overnight bank with madness. Took a gold stash, and lots of cash. With the powerful Hummer, we were ramming cars, bursting through steel bars. Then away we went, in a fast sprint.

Picked up by a satellite, as we racing in the night. Bailing through the signal light, across the intersections, leaving motorists without protection.

The Crew of Guns and Roses, sent shark waves through the city. Tearing through the streets without mercy, or pity.

Thundering across freeways, flashing down highways like lightning. At times it was frightening. Refusing to stop, leaving miles in the black top.

In a street chase, we wore mask on our face. Wrapped ourselves in body armor, to avoid a gun blast, or a midnight trauma.

Police flood lights dominated the skyline. We made ourselves hard to find.

Targeted by a helicopter, hovering in the sky. Down the expressway, we made the Hummer fly.

The operations was moving fast. We paused for a moment beneath an over pass, before proceeding through. To hide ourselves, from the eye of the helicopter's view.

Suddenly, we were pinned in with no escape. The cops seized the moment, and open fire.

A gun battle pursued, as though hails of bullets were raining from the sky. In a quest for the Crew to die.

We did not think that it would last long, but everything started to go wrong. The streets became a battle zone. Two cops went down, we knew there was no turning around.

The street were dripping with blood. Far into the night, the gun battle could be heard.

With powerful guns at our exposer, we tried to maintain our composure.

High power guns the cops were pumping. Under heavy fire we took a thumping.

A bullet enter my side. I felt as though I was going to die. A bleeding man, racked with pain. My mind was insane.

Two of the Crew members were blasted repeatedly. They cried out, but my ears were dead to their cry. I struggled to hang on, trying not to die.

A gloomy tomb. Two Crew members lives were doomed. They both turned toward the cops.
It was a first look, and a last good-bye, for their dying eyes.

Bidding them a farewell, may their souls, not burn in hell.

My wounds healed. My brother Zack, and I, are living on death row. To the electric chair, we will go.

Crime does not pay. I will advise the young men to live their lives in a honorable way.

Live a lawful life. Get a good education and marry a good wife.

Get a trade, or a profession. Take time to count your blessings. Hell is hot, be thankful, for what you got.

The Crew of Guns and Roses. Criminal minds, buried in the darkness of time.

LADY OF THE NIGHT

A lady of the night. Her beauty was
  As jewels to my sight. Wearing
    Diamonds and pearls. She
      Came into my empty world.

Out of the night, into my wasted
  Life, she came. Bearing a
    Moment of sweet relief.
      Than came misery and pain.

I fell in love with the lady of the
  Night. My heart feared that it
    Would not turnout right.

My sunshine was turned into rain.
  My nights were filled with madness,
    And can never be the same.

My mind struggled to seize control,
  But my heart had been left cold.
    Then came misery and pain.

I treated her as though she was
  A queen. One of the best,
    But she ripped my heart
      Right out of my chest.

Her lips were hiding the truth.
    Her eyes were bearing lies.
        Whence she never apologized.

My laughter has ceased. In the
    Confide of a woman's word
        I have lost belief.

Into my life she came. A lady of the
    Night. Wearing a smile without
    Shame. Bearing stinging love
        That has driven my heart insane.
            Then came misery and pain.

The love in my heart she has
    Decreased. Wherein the
    Moment of truth, I searched
        For peace, but all that remain,
            Is misery and pain.

THE VALLEY OF THE PUPPETS

In a remote corner of the world. There once was a place called, "The Valley of the Puppets."

Like puppets on a string. Men, women, and children were made to perform hard labor from day-to-day, for very little pay.

Open eyes, to an early rise. To wet fields, rolling meadows, and grasses hills, they were led. Just moments of crawling out of hard seats, and cold beds.

The people would awaken before sunrise, with sleepy eyes, standing in line to get a ride. Because of the grueling work, the days before, their bodies were still feeling tired.

At sunset, another hard day was complete, their duties had been met. They would scatter throughout the countryside. To reach their homes, when the day was gone.

Others would travel even farther, to reach the edge of town. Into the night they would lay their tired bodies down.

From sunrise; until dusk, the labor of their hands was never enough.

When the rain came, they would sometime get rest. The working hours would change. The children would get time to play games. To relieve the pain, the people welcomed the rain.

On Sundays, they would go to church. Attending Sunday

school first. Enjoying wonderful Sunday dinners. All through the
seasons, from the eyes of summer, to the endless coldness of winter.

They would work like slaves, beyond the tiny wages that they were paid. During the evening sunset, the river would turn a deep red. Reflecting the blood that workers had bled.

The people would work vigorously, before the rising of the morning sun.

When the sun went down, they would depart. Weaken by a grueling work day, right from the start. Beneath the scorching sun, they would work, till their faces were sun baked.

Puppets on a string. Manipulated by an evil hand. Doing hard time, for the man. Running tears, through the pages of the years. Their bodies grew weak and tired. No extra pay on the side.

When a child would graduate from high school. They would leave home, searching for a better place to belong.

Because of the untold misery, the writing was on the wall. the Valley of the Puppets, was doom to fall.

My name is Mike Jones. I was one of those people. A puppet on a string. A child, with tears in his eyes. By the strength of heaven, I was made to survive.

Along with my sibling, and other boys and girls. We would look toward the sky. Thinking of the future, and other ways to survive.

Puppets on a string. Birds on the wing. Wishes to fly far away, into a distant day. Away from the trying times, to a golden oasis, as our dreams reached out to find.

Where we could feel the warmth of the sunshine. Smell the aroma of apple blossoms, and fresh scented alpine.

Feel the gentle touch of the wind. Journey to colorful places, where our souls had never been.

In my teen years. I journeyed far from home. Other parts of the world, I would roam. I took odd jobs, sometime I would almost starve.

I learned to gamble. Playing for high stakes, from midnight, till daybreak.

My soul was weary and sad. I knew this kind of life would not last. The teaching from my childhood would reveal a sense of direction, that this way of life was wrong. Soon my money was gone.

I tried my hand at rock-and-roll, making music, singing a song, till the night was gone. Getting in fights, sweating under the spotlights, everything started to go wrong.

Traveling from city-to-city, living on the road. On my mental state of mind, this was a heavy load.

After a few years with the band, I cut my tides, and moved along, with no money in hand. I put music aside, with the future still before my eyes.

To the Valley of the Puppets, I returned. Moved back home, no other place to roam.

The Valley of the Puppets. Where wooden coffins lined the bottom of the cemetery. Where to many young men, had been buried.

It holds the spirits of the dead, who died working under a spell. Cast by a witch doctor, in the Valley of the Puppets, where they fell.

Performing the dance of death, beneath the full moon. To relieve the weak of their burdens. A ritual to remove pain, from the people hard working hands.

The conditions here shaped the lives of the people. The Valley of the Puppets, was marked by the dirt roads, flat farmland, and whitetail deer. The rich folk houses that sat on a hill, overlooking the rich green fields.

To relieve the grueling pain, inflicted by the long hard work days. I started a movement to set the people free. Soon I was lockup. They threw away the key.

As days went by, I manage to break free. My feet began to flee. I was a fugitive on the run. I found a way, to lay hands on powerful guns.

With vengeance on my mind. Back to the Valley of the Puppets, I once again returned. My feet refused to run.

Along with a few friends, we went underground. Traveling from city to town. Promising to fight to the end.

No more would we flee, we were destine to make the people free. We went on a rampage for days, trying to turn the page.

We hired Lawyers to plead our case. "No more long working days. Better working conditions in a day, and higher pay."

Going underground, we took an awful chance. No one could understand, the essence of our plan.

To obtain the money, for the Lawyers, and fight for a cost, we were at a lost. We went on a dangerous spree. Engaging in arm robbery, and other illegal dealings. Taking money, for the Lawyers fee.

We robbed armored cars. Knocked off various banks. At times, we would land behind jail house bars.

We knew this type of behavior was deadly. We could die at anytime, but at this juncture we didn't mind.

This criminal activity was not simply turning pages in a book. We knew how it looked, but we were geared, and did whatever it took.

The fires of our faith burn high. Whether we live, or die. Nevertheless, we contained our pride.

Giving our lives as sacrificial lams, for the freedom of many. Who will no longer have to work for pennies.

Some men have died, a vicious death. Right before my eyes. Shot down in cold blood. I barely survived.

Before the demise, of the Valley of he Puppets. Most people had moved away, despite receiving higher pay, and a decent work day.

I now set behind prison walls, day-after-day. Wondering if there was a better way, to have got the job done, or if I should have stayed on the run.

Lives were lost. I ask myself, was it worth the cost? Here I set. Lockup in a cold prison cell. My mind thrust into a dark spell. Living in the belly of hell.

Tell the young people out there, to be a better thinker than I. Take a stand, but get a good education, and have a well thought out plan.

Violence is not the key, peace it shall be. Now, my eyes can plainly see, as I live in misery. For me it is to late, never did I anticipate. Living behind prison walls, my soul is at a total lost.

The Valley Of The Puppets

VINTAGE FLASH

Bring back the
old sunshine,
wind and
roses.

The bright moon
light, that
painted the
sweet summer
nights.

Recall the sunny
days, and summer
places. Where
lovers would go,
for sunny
faces.

The winter winds,
where time has
been. The ways
we went, the
times we
spent.

Show me the
springtime
flowers, that
fluttered in
the morning
hours.

The green grasses
beneath the
rain showers.
The twinkling stars,
the old vintage
cars.

The love we
felt, when our
hearts would
melt.

The diamond
Ring, that made
our heart
sang.

Vintage flash, with a monster smash.

THE GHOST OF JEZEBEL

She came to me like an angel in the night, with a glow of black light.

She turned out to be a Ghost from hell, of the age gone by. Looking for a soul to sell.

The wind was in her hair. Her skin appeared to be young, and fair. Her name was Julie, my eyes were enchanted by her beauty.

She danced into my arms, I could not resist her charm.

A kiss in the night. When holding her tight, the Ghost from hell, robbed me of my sight.

My eyes could not see, that she was afraid of the light. She lived in darkness, her sins had never been pardoned.

She clawed her way into my heart, my life began to fall apart.

She spoke to me in a whisper. My ears could not understand, what her lips were saying. My heart could not avoid her evil plan.

My mind played tricks on me. With the beauty of her delightful face, she ravished me, for days.

When she departed, I felt broken hearted. My body lingered, from the effects of her evil ways. The moments she left me, her image would fad. My eyes could not remember, the appears of her face.

She would turn off the lights, but sleep would not come to her in the night.

She harbored the most evil ways, from the dark ages, taken from the burning pages.

I could feel her flames burning. Cutting into my soul like a dagger. Liken to a drunken man, my feet began to stagger.

She pretended to be a nurse. When I was in pain, she began to curst. Her eyes were ice cold, she had come for my soul.

When the morning came, she covered her face in shame. I was a confused man, my heart was racked in pain, my life would never be the same.

The night was lazy, it felt as though I was going crazy. The Ghost from hell, had no heart beat. Raw meat, she began to eat.

Suddenly, my body went cold. The ghostly shadow of Satan moved in close, pulling at my soul. In the confusion, my mind I was losing.

Satan, the enemy of man. The devil, at times identified as Lucifer, the chief of the fallen angels, pretending to be a stranger.

He came flying in, holding on to the east wind. Ready for

a fight, pulling me into the darkness, away from the light. Spreading evil deeds, planting corrupted seed.

He had sent the Ghost of Jezebel, straight up from the gates of hell. To steal my soul, and render my body ice cold.

My heart was heavy, and in doubt, but her cold love, I could not do without. My troubles were rising like a bad dream, with nothing in between.

Hammered by Satan, and tossed about.
Waiting for the exact moment, to rip my soul out.

The Ghost of Jezebel, straight up from the gates of hell. She brought with her an evil spell. Holding onto the passage of time, waiting to plant an evil seed, within my mind.

At the close of the day, my soul went astray. I was inflicted, running about, lost and turned out. Like a ghost living in darkness, prowling the night, running from the light.

A deep sleep fell upon my eyes, bitter dreams brought tears to cry.

The Ghost of Jezebel, robbed me of my money, Speaking words coated with honey.

Her claws dug deep into my sold, she began to remove my clothes.

The hard rain came, Satan was prowling the black night, evading the light. Roaming the back roads, in a fight to steal my soul.

I could see his shadow riding on the wind, there, he came creeping in.

His long black cape was hanging over his back, across his shoulders, floating on air. His red horns barely protruded from his long shaggy hair.

Thunder was exploding like bombs on a battle ground. Fire and lightning were sweeping across town.

He raised his face toward the sky. Hell fire was dripping from his eyes. Like a wild beast, he let go a loud roar. Shaking the structure of the city, like an earth quake. Showing no pity.

It echoed across the night, he came looking for a fight, hiding from the light.

Buildings came crashing down, falling to the rain soaked ground. The town folk were exploding with fright. They would run and hide, thinking they might die.

He was ducking, and dodging, to keep the light from his eyes. Only in darkness could he survive.

He was huge and tall. Crouching behind city walls, catching lightning with his paws.

Flinging it across the night, into the darkness, away from his sight.

He walked fast. His legs took long strides, moving in a glide. His huge feet tramped over barking dogs, nipping at his heels. The sight of him gave me the chills.

It had been foretold, that he was coming after my soul. My body would go cold, losing all control.

He carried a hairy hide, of a wild beast, to wrap my soul within. As to keep it in one piece, with punishment, for my sins.

The warm flames that burned in my body went with the wind. I had been living in sin. My life seem to be coming to an end. The inward eyes of my mind, had gone with the passage of time.

It was a stormy night, I had been robbed of my sight. Cast under a spell, by the Ghost of Jezebel, of the age gone by. Darkness was upon my eyes.

The wind blew fierce, cold as ice, cutting like a knife. I struggled for my life.

Satan face was against the sea, attempting to rob me of my soul. Using my unforgiving sins as a key. The blood in my veins was heavy, and cold.

Through a dry riverbed, I was led. To the sea we arrived, with darkness upon my eyes.

Blindfolded, carried back into the passage of time. The wind was rushing in. I was taken to a place where men had never been.

My body was strapped down, stretched across a raft. Crafted from logs of an old oak tree. Drifting slowly out to sea. Then, carried by a current, swiftly barreling through the deep waters, absent of deterrent.

The sea was cold, my body lost control. My burdens were of a heavy load.

A huge shadow, fell upon the waters. Bearing light from the stars. Fire began to burn from the depths of the sea, lighting up the night. Satan refused to fight.

He appeared to be obsessed. Pounding on my body, about to rip my soul, right out of my chest.

The moon came down closer, bearing light from the sky, from days gone by.

Three white doves, with wings of love, nestled by my side. Giving light to my eyes.

Warm rain showers fell upon the sea, washing my soul clean. The shadow on the water held the key, to set my soul free.

Minutes turned to hours, Satan began to lose his power. He trembled with fear, his eyes could not gaze upon, the shadow on the water, whose name was sealed.

Weaken by the light. He took flight, Bailing into the night. Back to the age gone by. Running from the eyes, in the sky.

Back to the ashes of hell, he fell. With the Ghost of jezebel.

THE LOVE FOR
HIS WOMAN

His lips, yearn for the kiss of
    Her sweet lips. His arms, long
        To hold her. His ears wishes to
Hear the tender words that she whisper, in times to remember.

His eyes desire to see her
    Beautiful face. To warm his
        Heart, in all his wasted days.
Each precious moment they spent, was heaven sent.

He love her, when the wind
    Blows. He love her, when
        The days are cold. Beneath
The full moon, He love her, in the midst of the afternoon.

Who can find a woman so lovely?
    A place beyond the stars, in the
    Vicinity of the planet Jupiter and mars.
        Is where you can find his love.
Shining bright as the sun. Before the day is done.

SABOTAGE

Sabotage, looming large. Broken dreams, and dying hearts. Into the world, forgotten boys, and girls. Dropping out of school, graduating to the streets, packing heat. Spilling blood, looking for love. Barely getting enough to eat.

Life and destruction. A Nation of corruption. Passing laws for just a few. Creating loopholes, with hearts that are cold, doing what they want to do.

Sabotage, living hard. The world is being ripped apart. Crumbing with greed. By those who are breaking the rules, in opposition, to the law, to take the lead. Killing to succeed.

Empty words, sounds absurd, for some boys and girls. Promised an education, still they are dropping out school, their lives are setup to lose. shrewd manipulation. Money, and time, are spent on someone else vacation.

Fighting some of the crime, dropping a dime. Are we doing our part? It is defiant, the young is still dying, living with bleeding hearts.

It's ashamed, hearts of burning pain, whose to blame. Dealing with an unclean hand.

Fathers and Mothers, are doing their best. Yet, they get no rest. Stabbed in the heart, their lives are destroyed. Struggling to survive, and refusing to die.

Sabotage, broken hearts. The streets are overrun with guns. Buy and sell, does anyone care? It's not like we are having fun.

Children are dying, all the time, from the barrels of guns. In a heavy load, guns are easily bought and sold. Yet, there are those, fighting in opposition, to gun control.

Life and destruction, raining down corruption. Young hearts looking for a good start. Manipulated; incarcerated. A mind scarred; a soul made hard.

Those who have an iron grip on the rules. A young mind they try to bruise, with nothing to lose.

Their sunshine buried itself into the darkness of night. Sabotage was their only fight. Hanging on till tomorrow, trying to climb out of sorrow.

Women and wine, They spend their time, playing with our minds. Exploding bombs, blazing guns, looking to have big fun.

A dazzling sunburst, at the winds they curst, going on a rampage for days, bucking for a hoax that pays. Stolen dreams, illegal schemes, Evading the law in evil ways.

Police brutality, is just a formality. A judge looks the other way. His arms are crossed, justice get lost, His iron fist reaches for higher pay.

Rulings against the broken hearts, those who are living in pain. Trying to survive, with watery eyes. Crying for the ones, sentence to die.

Sabotage, with a lightning rod. Pillars of fire, burning toward the sky, for our eyes to see. Flames of destruction, burning corruption, growing like the tallest tree, rising like the red sea.

A grin, and a smile. Nothing passes the saboteurs by. Staring into the rain clouds, their thunder roars aloud. Evading the lightning strikes, running form the big payback.

Sabotage, living large. Dealing in blood money, and gold bars. Soon, they will be pumping iron on a prison yard.

Playing dangerous games with death row cards. Living with a mind that has fallen apart.

An enemy agent, many lives they have wasted. Searching to avoid the time they are facing.

On a dark day, They are sentence to die. Yet, they have managed to squeeze by. Harboring deceitful plans, to escape doom, before their awaiting tomb.

Injury and destruction. To many lives have been lost. Saboteurs will be doing time, setup to please the big boss.

Making deals with the devil, never on the level. Engaging in sabotage, at home and abroad, in stormy weather. Where criminal minds come together.

Sabotage, falling stars. Thrust onto a prison yard. Shackled and chained, a condemned man, have a date with death. Waiting for the howling moon, it will come soon.

THE HANGMAN'S
CALLING

It was late in the evening, at the end of a grueling day. The glow of the sunset had melted away. The edge of twilight was on display.

A full moon was hanging high above the dead of night, glowing with fading light.

The stars in the sky, were nestled behind the dark clouds as they sailed by.

Young men were paraded out to the tall Hangman's Gallows. Delivered up to be hang by the neck until they were dead, by a man named, "Parry Dallas." There, they were led to the gallows.

Every month, on the last Friday of the month. Murderous, and other violent criminals were condemned to die. They were to speak their final good-by, beneath the night sky.

Years ago, the economy had been slow. A drought had stricken the land. Jobs were not plentiful. Hired hands were sent home, looking for other places to roam.

Parry Dallas, was a married man. His family depended on the labor of his hands. The drought had broken his spirit. He had no plans, his heart was weary.

He left home to find work, traveling long distances abroad, far and wide. The land was barren before his eyes.

In a far off land, he took a job as a Hangman. The only job he could find, it was the worst of times.

Men lined up for the Hangman's job. Many were called to speak, for this job to seek. As the day was closing, Parry Dallas, was chosen.

When it was time to carryout his duty, he kept stalling, but this job was his calling.

He would hang men high, they were doom to die. Fire and light was gleaming in the night, Torches, and candles lit up the site. The only matter left, were the condemned men awaiting to die, a quick death.

Beyond the doors of the shadows, and darkness, mysterious bloodhounds would breakout barking.

Near a sacred place, that held old tails of the fallen. Once a year, the spirits of the dead, would have their names read.

Parry Dallas, was lost in the drama of the moment. Everything seemed to be moving fast, when out of the days of time, came a page out of the past.

Bitter dreams had raced through his mind, of his long lost family, he had left behind.

The day was chilled, and the wind was still. The sky was angry. Sadness laced the air, as one man's sentence had been unfair.

He was delivered up to die, tears rolled down his eyes.

He was led up the steps to the tall gallows. There, to be hang by the neck until he was dead. Carried out by the Hangman, Parry Dallas.

On this day, men had fallen to their death, through the gallows gate. Thrust into their fate.

The Hangman's bell would sound. Moments later the dead ,would be stretched across the cold hard ground.

Beneath the open sky, the night seemed to come alive. Packing a big surprise.

To the top of the Hangman's gallows the young man was led. A black sack was placed over his head. His hands were tired. On this day he was to die, and say his last good-by.

The Hangman, Parry Dallas, moved about the gallows. Suddenly, his hand began to shake. His body began to sweat, and his clothes became soaking wet.

The crowd stared in amazement. The condemned criminals, they thought none were worth saving. Words were at a hush. No one would say much.

Parry Dallas, placed the Hangman's noose around the young man's neck. The gallows controls seemed to be set.

Atop the tall structure, Parry Dallas walked around, twirling his hands, and staring down, at the ground.

Then came a loud roar of thunder. The people began to wonder. Lightning strikes swept across the site. Eyes could see the black sky hanging over the night.

An innocent man was about to die, right before the people eyes. Through the years, Parry Dallas heart, had harden. In this case he was filled with a sense of pardons.

He was fierce, in his skill. An innocent man, he did not wish to kill.

In an instant, a lightning strike swept across the Hangman gallows, slicing through the Hangman's body. Sending fire of spirits deep down into his soul, that had once grown cold.

He raised his hands, and lift his head high, toward the black sky. Tears were rolling down his eyes.

He bellowed a loud cry. "Save this man, here and now, as I stand. He is an innocent man.
I can feel his pain, as though we are one of the same." His hands trembled in fear, this man he could not kill.

Swiftly, the gallows gate open, the young man dropped. Swinging in midair, as no one cared.

Hanging at the end of the Hangman's rope, suddenly, the rope broke. Parry Dallas, cut it with a knife, to save the young man's life.

He removed the black sack from the young man's head, then away he fled. Confused, in his state of mind, wondering had this man been abused, and had others been unfairly accused.
Again he began to run. To the gallows he returned. In a loud voice, a soul cry out from beneath the gallows. "This young man is your son."

The black clouds were rolled away. The darkness of night was approaching day.

Parry Dallas, slowly turned around, removed himself from the ground. Weak and in pain, dirt covered his face and hands. With tears in his eyes, the young man he saved, was his child.

A sight before the people eyes, they both began to cry. His long lost son, out of all his children, his eyes gazed upon only one.

Parry Dallas realized, that had he not been hired as a Hangman. His beloved son would have died. It appeared that the world all around him was falling. This endeavor was the Hangman's calling.

He traveled back to his home, where he once belong. His wife, and he, lived happily. The children are all grown, and have moved on, with families of their own.

Parry Dallas, lived to save the bones, of his bones. Blood, of his blood. Creating for them, a happy home.

A HEART OF GOLD

He had a heart
of gold. Born
deep into
his soul.

People who wore
shaggy rages,
he would
give them
clothes.

He would put
shoes on
their
feet.

When they were
hungry. He
would give
them food
to eat.

A neighbor
in need, he
tries to
please.

A distant friend,
whose luck may
have come to

an end. Money
he would
send.

A struggling man.
He would extend
a helping
hand.

Those who have failed
to succeed. Brought
to their knees.
He is a friend
indeed.

From his heart
he gave, lives
he have saved.
Leaving no
room for
disgrace.

A man of sunshine.
A man of no
shame. Who
can stop
the rain?

A heart of gold, deep down in his soul.

THE HITCHHIKER

The Hitchhiker, thumbing for a ride. Awaiting
a motorist, may none pass me by. To get
away, into the distant day. No
money to pay. The rise of a
thumb, who
will come.

Traveling abroad, the freeway is clogged. My
only possessions are the clothes on my
back, the things stuffed in my back pack.
Searching eyes, spying for a
ride. who will pass me by.
A walk for a
miles.

Into another town, watching the sun go down.
A place to slumber, a room without a
Number. A calm I have found. A
hard bed without a pillow.
Yet, my sleep will be
sound.

Wind in my face, running for days. Beneath the
blue sky, thumbing for a ride. Burning
dreams, as flames of fire urge me on.
The Hitchhiker, looking
for a place to
belong.

Dancing in the wind, singing to the sky, looking
for a way to please my wandering eyes.
Dancing in the night, blinded by
the light. A tanned face,
touched by the sun
baked days.
Sundown, all around, before the midnight
sounds. Walking miles into the next
town. Tonight my bed will be
made on the cold
ground.

Sunrise, open eyes. Wandering beneath
the blue sky. A little slumber, a
little rest, I confess, no one
to caress. Hitching a ride,
A little sleep for
my weary
eyes.

      The Hitchhiker ,
           thumbing for
               a ride.

REVENGE OF THE BLACK HAWKS

It was a late afternoon. The sun would be going down soon. Black Hawks had been spotted zooming into town, making agitated sounds. Coming out of the sky. Flying across the mountain top, with madness in their eyes.

In what seemed to be a hidden world. A scene came alive. Right before the town folk eyes, who stood nearby.

The Hawks flew into town with wings of terror, spread across the winds. Looking for a man who had done some of the Black Hawks in. Plowing through the cold air, seeking sweet revenge.

Stalking the city in a rage, with death in their face. The notorious Black Hawks, were ready for a vicious attack, with a lightning strike.

With their sharp beaks, they were prone to kill, without reluctance or fear.

They arrived on the scene, mad and mean. Ready to render themselves as supreme.

The sky was red. The Black Hawk Nation had just finished putting away their dead. Killed by a man named, "Delbert Peterson."

He blasted the birds with a shotgun loaded with buckshot. as they sat in the trees, playing among the winter leaves.

They came looking for revenge, with a scheme to bring Peterson life to an end.

They flew across town, in search of Delbert Peterson, but he was nowhere to be found. They
waiting atop buildings, in trees and among the weeds. In hope that Peterson would show his face. He they wanted to waste.

It appeared that their eyes reflected flames of fire. Birds of a feather, ready for any kind of weather. The Black Hawk Nation, Flying in formation, hanging together.

It had been said that these Hawks had the brain of a man. That if you speak to them in a certain voice they would understand.

They cried out in agony, with hearts of pain. They had lost a huge part of their family, and were calling out the wanted man.

Delbert Peterson, would have to pay, for the killings of the Black Hawks before the break of day.

The sun had went down, melted into the shade of darkness. The Black Hawks were still waiting around. The moon sat above the night. Reflecting rays of black light.

They occupied the city streets, in the small country town. Delbert Peterson, refused to come around.

They took to the sky, with wings flying high. In hopes of spotting Peterson, before the night passes by.

Patiently awaiting, beneath the dark moonlight, headed into midnight.

The town folk began to talk. The Black Hawks listened to the words they were saying. With sharp brain power, words they would understand.

Suddenly, with their keen minds, in a short span of time. The Black Hawks got a clue into where Peterson was staying. By the words, the town folk, had spoke.

The Black Hawks flew high, as the moon, and the stars reflected rays of black light, across the night sky.

It was just a little while, until they spotted the house, that sat at the edge of town. Peterson dwelling place, they had found.

The air was warm and sluggish. It hung heavily over the house, of Delbert Peterson, the louse.

The Hawks came out of the sky, from the distant night. You could see the madness in their eyes. As they were geared for a fight.

They surrounded Peterson house, with sounds of a loud cry. Calling for Peterson, to bring his body outside.

Some hovered in midair, the town folk stood and stared. Peterson laid low. Outside of his house, he was afraid to go. He felt safe inside, but there was no place to run, no place to hide.

A regiment of the Black Hawks Nation, traveled to a nearby coal mine. With torches, the mine was aligned.

With their powerful beaks, they grabbed the torches, with flames of hot fire. They took to the sky, when the night was nearing it's peak. The killer of Black Hawks, they were geared to defeat.

The flames burned high, beneath the black sky, giving light to their eyes.

Back to the Peterson place they would fly. Lighting up the sky. The torches burned bright. Into the night.

The Black Hawks were angry. They were ready for Peterson to come out, and fight, before the morning light.

They hovered above the Peterson house, bearing the torches with feet and mouth, that lit up the site, as they arrived.

The town folk assembled, and stared. The red hot torches continued to flare, heating up the night air.

They dropped the flaming torches on top of the house. Fire begin to burn sky high. Burning up the night, cutting through the light.

Suddenly, Delbert Peterson, came out running fast. He was ablaze, He ripped his clothes from his body. Agony showed on his face. Racing through the night, at a very fast pace.

The Black Hawks gave chase, flying low. Closing in on Peterson. He ran as fast, as he could go.

The Hawks wanted him dead, as they flew in close striking at his head. Fire, and blood gleamed in their eyes. With wings of revenge they would fly.

The town folk followed like a mob. Making noise, and leaving their jobs. An attempt to lend a hand, to get the thing resolved.

Delbert Peterson, had two brothers, who came with guns. Their intention was to shot, and kill the Black Hawks until there were none.

Outside of the city limit. The Hawks had Delbert Peterson surrounded. He was looking for a place to run, but could not find none.

The brothers began firing their shotguns. The town folk would scatter and run. As the Hawks tried to get the job done.

Peterson brothers, shot innocent bystanders. They were evil men, but their lives would soon be coming to an end.

The Black Hawks would fly high, into the sky. Circling around the men, waiting for the right moment to zoom in.

A huge fire was ignited, the Hawks continue to stalk. The fire burned high, almost touching the sky.

Delbert Peterson was seen standing on a rock, above a mountain top. Water transformed into steam, at the bottom of a hot pit. Peterson eyes gazed upon the place, where the flames were lit.

The clouds that hung over the site were black as coals. The night was dim, and the moon was bold.

Delbert Peterson, stumble and fell into a river of fire. Over a tall steep cliff, his body drift.

He was last see stretched across a hot rock. The rhythm of his heart had stopped. He landed below. Whether his body was found, no one knows.

The town folk attacked the two brothers with stones, until all the life from their bodies, was gone.

The remainder of Black Hawk Nation, flew away, before the next day. They took to the sky, with burning flames in their eyes. On a night when men, and Black Hawks, were doomed to die.

MASQUERADE

He lived his life behind a masquerade. Hiding his true
feeling as he
went through
his lonely
days.

His heart had been broken. He went through life
laughing and
joking. Wearing
a masquerade
over his
face.

His face seemed to be smiling, but his heart could
not ceased crying.
Disguising his
ways behind a
masquerade.

He attended parties, and balls, at the finest halls. There,
he was at peace. No
one could see, the
tears that fell down
his face. When
he hid behind a
masquerade.

Reluctant to remove it. He wore it wherever he went.
a social gathering,
a political event.
Bearing a broken
Heart, wherever he
was sent.

With a painful heart. He wore his masquerade right
from
The start. When
the night life
came alive. This
was the way he
survived.

Hiding his disgrace. Longing for the woman he once
Embraced. Her
wine he would lace.
As he hid behind
his masquerade.
Drinking a portion,
lost in his
emotions.

BULLET TRAIN

Men, women, girls and boys. Hear the
message that flows from my voice. Pouring
out of my soul.

Like cool spring waters, that give life to the
wild flower, awaiting the spring showers.

You have been foretold, the history of the
underground railroad. How the life, and
time of a people played out, and unfolded.

How male and female broke free, from
a life of misery. From the shackles and
chains, that bound them to a world of
pain.

Deep into the distance of time. The heirs
of a lasting bloodline of a people, who
remain.

Come together, and create a high speed
Bullet Train.

To travel across the rolling plains. Into the
land of higher education. Where dreams,
and hopes will emerge as a preservation.

Design it with the love, and compassion
that flowed from the old underground
railroad.

Created by both men, and women. Black
and white, running in the night.

Who gave a gift of sacrifice. To bridge the
way to an escape, for freedom sake.
To take flight, out of the darkness of night.

Journey into a land overflowing with
wisdom, knowledge, and understanding.

With protection and directions, enabling
the train to move at speeds of a safe
selection. Into a world of affection.

With the fruits of courage that our
ancestors once grew, and the work they
chose to do. Like Harriet Tubman, and
Sojourner Truth.

Soar above the highest peaks. Sail across
untamed rivers and lakes. Conquer the
future we seek. Explore a world of new
opportunities.

Filled with endless wonders of delight.
Take the Bullet Train to the land of lasting
love, and higher education. The future will
be extremely bright.

Where eyes can see the beautiful dreams
that falls like snow, from the heavens to the
green valleys below.

Speed across the sandy plains, aboard the
high speed Bullet Train.

Across the highest mountains to the west.
The rolling hills to the east. In the land of
plenty, and have a victory feast.

Leave behind all destructive behavior.
Develop talents, skills, and careers.
Creating an everlasting favor.

Journey to a world of a different kind.
Leaving the killing of our sisters and
brothers far behind.

Eradicating the evil deeds of unforgivable
crime. Leaving behind the lost days, where
taking a life was a terrible waste.

Where violence was the wrong call, and
ignorance landed many behind prison
walls.

Live wisely, and choose education
over incarceration. Choose to stop the
bloodshed, be a friend instead.
A solemn oath. We must take! Before we
board the high speed Bullet Train. That

will lives in our hearts and souls. At all times, imprinted in the archives of our minds.

An oath, that we shall not spill the blood of any humankind. Nor harbor wicked intentions, or create evil inventions.

Obey the law of the land, and have no malice, or animosity toward any woman or man. This will be our oath, that we will honor throughout all the land.

Journey to a new land with vibrant waves of colors, with refreshing meadows, and flowing streams, that mends broken dreams.

Follow the lead of those who were cool, and stayed in school. Progressed into a world of success, earn respect, and have no regrets.

Like those who have kept their families together as a unit of one, and those who have effectively raised their daughters and sons.

Became successful in a career, or a chosen field.

Create this high speed Bullet Train to fly
with wings, or as a vessel that sails, as if the
wheels never touch the rails.

Bringing people together in the land of
higher education. Where the morning
shines a vivid bright, in a land of success.
Where the future will radiate with the
brightest sunlight.

Travel into tomorrow under the flying
red, white, and blue. All humankind are
invited, and so are you. To the land of
prosperity, in a time of clarity.

Journey beneath the wings of summer. Out
of the winter snow, through a rainbow of
flowers.

With the knowledge to empower. treasures
of possession, a career of profession.

An adventure to an oasis of luxury, leaving
a lasting impression.

Speed into the purpose of life, cutting
across the northern hemisphere, like a
sharp knife.

Moving through the exit plain. Away from
the lingering pain.

It will be a journey of many lifetimes. Mending broken hearts, and creating new dreams, as fresh as the running waters of valley springs.

Where dreams will come true. When the sun come shining through.

The Bullet Train will move with raw speed. On a fast track, at a time to be set. Charting a new course. Moving forward with the sound of a jet.

Across the icy slopes, into a land of ecstasy, and wings of hope. It will take you to a place of better days. Into a time to be embraced.

Gather if you may. On a mild summer day. Come aboard, if you can afford. If you desire to go for the ride, standby. The command, you will understand.

Open your eyes, so you can see. The creation of the high speed Bullet Train, and the green valleys of your destiny.

Unlocking a world of joy, and delight. Where colorful opportunities, and living dreams will blossom before your very sight.

Cruise into a world of eternal happiness.
Singing new lyrics of love. Beneath a
galaxy of stars, hanging from the blue sky
above.

Cruise into a land of plenty. Where
jealousy, and envy has been erased, from
the window of the minds.

Journey from the past, into a new and
present time. In a world of fairness, and
awareness.

Where dreams are realized, and blossom
beyond the sky.

Where hopes, and admirations are not
tossed aside. That can lead to better health,
and new found wealth.

The past is not dead. It lives on in our
hearts, souls, and minds.

Reflecting in the winds of time. Like the
rain showers, that brings beautiful dancing
flowers.

In the fading twilight hours. A beauty to
behold, with eyes of the soul. Come out
of the rain, and get aboard the high speed
Bullet Train.

PRIVATE EYE

Private Eye, I Spy, a man for hire. Slade, is my name.
Investigation is my game. Fighting organized crime, in hard
times.

I solve homicides. Any case where someone has died.
Manslaughter, made to order. Roaming the dangerous
streets of the cities, for the criminal, I have no pity.

I have investigated cheating husbands, and wives.
Uncovered clues, for those who have lost their lives.

I work along, in a field where anything can go wrong. At
times, I dress up in a disguise, so as to keep my identity
unknown. In the game of I Spy.

It is easy to lose your life. To someone, with a smoking gun.
A man on the run, or with the slash of a knife.

If you let your defense down, or relax. You might get a stab
in the back. In a second, your life could vanish, by the use
of a makeshift weapon.

I have investigated illegal back room deals. Where things
went wrong. Men were killed,
for someone else thrill.

As a Private Eye. I find ways, to make a case come alive.
Break it wide open, in a matter of days. For me, it comes
naturally, like a sea of waves.

Dangerously and deadly. It is no fun, that is why I carry a gun. I don't give up, until a clue is found, or until the perpetrator is brought down.

Black marketeers will take you out. So as to do their business, evading any chance of a living witness. committing fraud, at home and abroad.

I have solved cases where the wives have had their husbands killed physically, or mentally. To collect a huge insurance policy.

Husbands have had their wives kidnapped. Then arranged for someone else to take the wrap.

A case where the husband reported his wife missing. In the end, I discovered that her body, had been buried in the walls of his kitchen.

There is no room for error, in the unforgiving world of undercover. Where the days are filled with trouble. There are enemies within, and enemies without. If you make the wrong move, the game is over. They will take you out.

It is a hard job out here. Sleeping in the day, working for minimum pay. Prowling like a stray cat, in the dead of night. Keeping out of sight. At any moment, you may be engaged in a fierce fight.

Death and destruction, falls like rain, on the head of a Private Eye man. Sometimes I think I'm insane, living in a world filled with pain.
I have been shot five times. In the arm, leg, back, and head.

Once I was shot in the face. Laid up in a hospital for days. Trouble seem to leap from the sky, when you live a life, as a Private Eye.

At times, it appears that my life is wasting away. I press on, but then again, I have to get away, into the stillness of a day.

Tonight I'm investigating a bloody case of robbery gone bad, and three of the worse killings, this town has ever had.

It took place at Manhattan West. A department store that had a security system, that was one of the best.

I infiltrated an alley behind the large department store. Encountering two men who carried a sawed off shotgun, and a semiautomatic handgun.

I was disguised as a drunken Sailor, who had lost his way, just wandering through the day.

"Hey Sailor, what's up fool? What are you doing back here? Are you lost, or something?" One of the men asked.

"No, I'm cool." I replied. As I straggled nearby.

"Give me a cigarette, yo." One of the men said. "Why are you back here, in this dark alley all along? Aren't you scared?" He said.

"No, I'm not scared." I replied. "I'm looking for a friend, this is the place where we had been. I thought he might be coming back again." Is what I said.

Suddenly, I reached into my coat pocket, to grab a cigarette. Before I could pull it out, I was grabbed around my neck, and put in a chokehold. The perpetrators were mean and bold.

A semiautomatic weapon was pointing straight for my head. I thought I would soon be dead.

"Hold on a minute." I said. "I'm just getting a cigarette for you. Let go of my head."

As he let me go, I went into a flow, with a resounding blow. Then a roundhouse kick to the chest. I tried my best, to strike him in the head, instead. He was laid out, as I moved about.

Shots rang out. Bullets came flying pass me, from the other suspect. I quickly dove to the deck. I swiftly pulled my gun, and rolled to cover. I was about to pop one, or the other.

I got off a shot. Hitting the gun toting man in the shoulder. In an instant the battle was over. I summoned the cops. The two men, I had dropped.
They were tried, and convicted of the crime.

They are both setting on death row, living on the low. Soon they will say their last good by, before it is time to fry.

As time went by, I infiltrated a notorious smuggling ring. Men and women who participated in a thieving gang.

They smuggled human cargo, narcotic, robbed rich homes.

When the owners were gone.

I engaged in a gun battle along with the cops. The smuggling ring, we were destined to stop.

The night was moving about. The stars were hanging out. The night owls had played their final love tune, beneath the fading moon. Rays of light, had drifted far into the night.

We were informed that the smuggling ring was held up in a empty warehouse, outside of town. We moved in, ready to take them down.

With lights flashing, and sirens blasting, we quickly arrived on the scene. We knew the ring was dangerously mean.

We called out to the Perpetrators, using a bullhorn, then sent in a telephone, moving right along.

"Come out with your hands up, and no one will get hurt." We were alert, as we tried to reason with the smuggling ring, to carryout a sting.

"Throw out your guns, nobody try to run, or we will have to shoot you down, using lightning rounds."

Inside the warehouse no one said a word, at least, none that I heard. "Do you understand, what we are saying? Makeup your mind, you don't have plenty of time."

They began firing shots none stop. Coming from inside

the warehouse, and from the top. We fired back. The perpetrators were not about to relax.

Suddenly, members of the smuggling ring were shot down. Others tossed their gun out, on to the ground.

We went in with powerful guns, sending them on the run. Right into the barrels of our outside guns.

We grabbed money that had been paid, for illegal slaves, setting them free. Members of the smuggling ring were taken into custody, others would flee.

To the slums, they would run. Abandoning their high rise, looking for a place to hide.

As time moved on, I was called upon to investigate the breaking and entering of rich homes. An easy target for looters, when the owners were gone.

It was a night of total darkness. The moon had disappeared from the dead of night. The galaxy of stars had refused to shine bright.

I was staking out a house. Feeling alive, I waited inside. I wore an infrared light, for visual in the night.

I waited in an upstairs room. I heard the sound of a window being smashed. To get a better look, down the stairs I dashed. I try to keep a routine, when I arrive on a crime scene.

I noticed four mask men crawling through the broken window, as I remember.

"Let's split up. We are looking for anything of value, including guns. So let's have some fun." Said one.

"There is lot's of stuff here, including money and gold, I have been told." Proclaimed one of the thieves. From downstairs I began to leave.

I took cover in an upstairs room. On the night of the fading moon.

The thieves scattered upstairs, and downstairs. At times moving in pairs.

I eased out, into the hall, to get a better look. I came Face-to-face, with a crook. Brandishing his weapon. I was on the hook. To remedy this situation, I would have to do whatever it took.

He raised his gun, I was stunned. He fired behind my back, carrying a heavy pack.
I dropped to the floor, homing in on the target, I fired back, with a precise strike. "Bang! Bang!" Black smoke billowed from my gun. I had took out the first one. Again I dropped down. My 44 magnum made a mean sound.

The thief took two rounds, tumbled to the bottom of the stairs, not going nowhere. He had been put down.

Suddenly! A myriad of gunfire was coming my way. I was in deep trouble, and began to pray. It occurred to me, that I may be living in my last day.

I moved behind a closet door, to reload, my 44. "Let's take a stroll, ready to rock-and-roll," is what I said. The thieves were pumping lots of hot lead. I had been in this kind of mess before. I pull myself together, to take the stroll, ready to rock-and-roll.

I kicked open the door, and came out blasting. "Bang! Bang! Bang!!!" I dove to the floor, and began blasting evermore. Into the night, two men fled. On the living room floor, another lay dead.

I summoned the men in blue, soon they would come through. I could see their flashing lights as they came. My body was racked in pain. In my back, I felt a burning. My head seemed to be turning.

I had taken two slugs. One to my back, the other to the side of my neck. As I tried to put the situation in context.

The fleeing suspects were captured running in the night.
They continued to put up a hard fight.
They took no time to pause, looking for a big payoff.
Venting their frustrations in drugs and crime, they will now be doing hard time.
As time went by, my wounds healed. I continued to work in the law enforcement field.

In the line of duty, many men have I killed. It is not a thrill. At times, when it cross my mind, I get a cold chill.

Many times I have bled. I could be dead. Into a dark cold grave, my body, could have laid.

This job is tough, but someone has to do it. It was my will, to enter, the law enforcement field.

This is the way my life turned out to be. Living the life as a Private Eye, is my destiny.

DREAMS FROM THE NIGHT

Dreams from the night. When gentle
    Arms held me tight. A little slumber
    Fell upon my eyes. Dreamy visions
        Begin to rise, passing through my mind,
        With shadows of designs, from the faces of time.

Mystic colors flashes through
    My head, of yellow, blue, and
        A shade of red. As I lay upon
          the pillows placed in my bed.

Dreams that stays alive, with wings
    To fly. Floating across the night sky,
        With stars of dreamy scenes. Flickering
        Before my sleeping eyes.

Dreams from the night. As doves
    Fly beneath the bright moonlight.
        Dreams that melt souls,
          When the cool wind blows.

Dreams that find the way into
    The ocean breeze, sails across the
    Mighty seas. Takes on a cycle of
        Patterns, that reaches across the
          Planets of Mar, Venus, and Saturn.

Dreams of spring fun, across
	The rich green fields. Where
	We use to run. Dreams that
		Rises in the atmosphere, with
			Images like clear crystal chandeliers.

Dreams from the night. That echo
	Memories of magnificent sites.
	A page out of the past. Illuminating
		Seasons of laughter, and the
			Good times that we had.

Dreams that lingers among the
	Rivers and lakes. Fantasies of lovely
	Journeys we long to take. Dreams
		Of laughing eyes, and charming smiles.
			Reflecting the wonders of days gone by.

		Dreams from the night,
			When gentle arms held me tight.

ENTER THE STORM

Enter the storm, whence
The fierce winds blow.
Rising up in rage,
Growling down
Below.

Where the mad rain, beats
Upon the plains.
howling like a
Beast, that's
Untamed.

Hear the thunder roar.
As the storm rip up
Trees, and steal
Leaves, as
It goes.

See the flashing lightning,
Striking flames of fire.
Blazing the sites,
Lighting up the
Night.

Where the air is freezing cold,
And the wind is mean and
Bold. Being unkind,
Roaring like
A lion.

Bouncing across rivers and
Lakes. Slithering through
Like a snake. Holding
Together stormy
Weather.   Enter The Storm